grids for the **dynamic image**

tanja diezmann & tobias gremmler

AVA Publishing SA
Switzerland

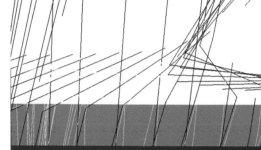

An AVA Book
Published by AVA Publishing SA
rue du Bugnon 7
CH-1299 Crans-près-Céligny
Switzerland
Tel: +41 786 005 109
Email: enquiries@avabooks.ch

Distributed by Thames and Hudson (ex-North America)
181a High Holborn
London WC1V 7QX
United Kingdom
Tel: +44 20 7845 5000
Fax: +44 20 7845 5055
Email: sales@thameshudson.co.uk
www.thamesandhudson.com

Distributed by Sterling Publishing Co., Inc.
in USA
387 Park Avenue South
New York, NY 10016-8810
Tel: +1 212 532 7160
Fax: +1 212 213 2495
www.sterlingpub.com

in Canada
Sterling Publishing
c/o Canadian Manda Group
One Atlantic Avenue, Suite 105
Toronto, Ontario M6K 3E7

English Language Support Office
AVA Publishing (UK) Ltd.
Tel: +44 1903 204 455
Email: enquiries@avabooks.co.uk

ISBN 2-88479-008-X

10 9 8 7 6 5 4 3 2 1

Concept & Design by
Tanja Diezmann and Tobias Gremmler

Text by Tanja Diezmann
Motion Graphics by Tobias Gremmler

All content by pReview digital design Gmbh, Berlin
www.pReview-design.com

English translation by Victor Dewsbery, Berlin
and Richard Holmes, Berlin

Production and separations by
AVA Book Production Pte. Ltd., Singapore
Tel: +65 6334 8173
Fax: +65 6334 0752
Email: production@avabooks.com.sg

table of content

table of content

introduction

introduction

Grids for the Dynamic Image is a book on grid systems for digital and dynamic media. It is aimed at professional media designers and applications such as television, the Internet, convergence media and devices. Every designer working in the field of digital media knows that »digital design« is extremely dynamic in every respect, and its rules are still very unchartered. This is not only a matter of appearance, but also of dynamics and interaction. Much of the knowledge applied at work every day has been accumulated the hard way in a lengthy process of trial and error. This book offers an insight into some of the methods developed over years of design work for the digital media.

The design of media content has become one of the fundamentals of our information society. Whether we think of television, the Internet, or mobile devices, the content is always presented visually, so that it needs to be given a graphical form. This can even go so far that the media themselves take over the role of presentation and explanation of contents, so that there is no longer any need for human moderation. We can already see this trend on television and the Internet.

Even the interfaces that offer us access to the digital world are graphically designed and become increasingly dynamic. They are becoming more and more important. In future, the design of digital features will decide the success of information transfer and is thus a key component of successful business.

At the same time, there is a need to gain more expertise regarding the design of moving images. Whereas classic design had many centuries to develop and generate its own rules, the existence of »digital design«, and in particular »motion graphics«, has only had a few decades to investigate the rules of the medium. In contrast to films, it is not about telling stories, but visualising contents and processes – visual communication.

The designer of the contents must know how to design a message so that it comes across properly and is understood. This involves the well-known Sender-Receiver model. Time plays an important role, and with it dramaturgy – the way contents and media are introduced over time, and the sequence of events. Dramaturgy is one, or even the crucial factor that decides whether an animation will seem interesting or boring, whether it will attract the attention of the viewers, or not.

Here again it is noticeable that the new media have not been around for so long and that most professional designers have learned through experience, and by trial and error. To some extent, of course, it is possible to learn from other media, but in the final analysis, the digital world operates under its own constraints and offers its own unique opportunities. Motion graphics usually involves graphics or typography that are combined together or integrated with real footage.

If graphics are integrated, then this involves artificial compositions that follow a »rule« created by the designer. Relevant features include the colour scheme, the form, the contrast, the movement and the dynamics, as well as the overall dramaturgy. It is the dramaturgy that finally determines where, when and how the graphics are dynamic, what rhythm they follow, and how they are used to guide the attention of the viewer.

In this context, grids are nothing more than the rules governing the dramaturgy, the rules that all design elements follow. They are very different from the grids used in classical design, primarily because they not only affect the placement and appearance of graphic elements, but also their behaviour, as well as the interaction of all components over time. This is used to generate dramaturgy and rhythm.

The grid systems are not only generated by dividing up the surface, but also by dividing up time and space. Certain elements are assigned to appear at a specific point of time and given their own dynamic characteristic. This can be created by a variety of methods, whether by hand, by setting individual key frames, or by transferring parameters from one element to another – tracking.

The methods of tracking can be created in very different ways for dramaturgy and design grids. By the manual transfer of parameters from one object to another, this object can then be controlled. For example, the movement patterns of one object might function as an animation grid for another object. The result is that the animations can be made to seem more natural, and since the behaviour is also derived from real footage, typography for example can follow the rhythm of the spoken word.

This mode of operation developed from the opportunities offered by digitalisation. Sound, image and animation programs operating digitally make it possible to exchange and transfer data and formats. This has made possible the development of cross-media approaches that bring with them the transfer of practices from one area to another.

Recently, software applications have been following this trend. Animation and 3D programs now usually have integrated tools, for example for transferring behaviour or expressions. Pre-defined options are provided, with parameters and links that can be manipulated. Automatic linking of two or more elements is possible, so that their behaviour can easily be controlled over time. The current development in digital design is towards the generation of dramaturgy through the behaviour, with more practicable control options.

The behaviour of graphic elements in animations has meanwhile almost taken on the character of identity. The trend here is now towards using dynamics and method to create an identity that is the same for all presentations. The nature of the animation is the identifiable element and characteristic for the message.

This will establish itself sooner or later in interactive media. After all, an interface is in principle a dialogue partner and not just a static screen. It is a character that just like a human presents itself with form and behaviour. For example, with an appropriate profile and self-contained behaviour, the navigation or the navigation model can have their own characters, that are defined by behaviour and not by form. Behaviour becomes the Brand. Graphics can follow current trends just like fashion.

This book provides an introduction to various methods of using dynamic grids and ways of generating them.

chapter and title
with chapter navigation which shows all other topics in a linear order.

abstract
presents the content of the page in one sentence.

stills
and sequences of the example animation are shown as a result of working with the presented grid.

graphics
visualise the principle of the grid.

text
explains how the grid works and how it was used in the presented motion graphic.

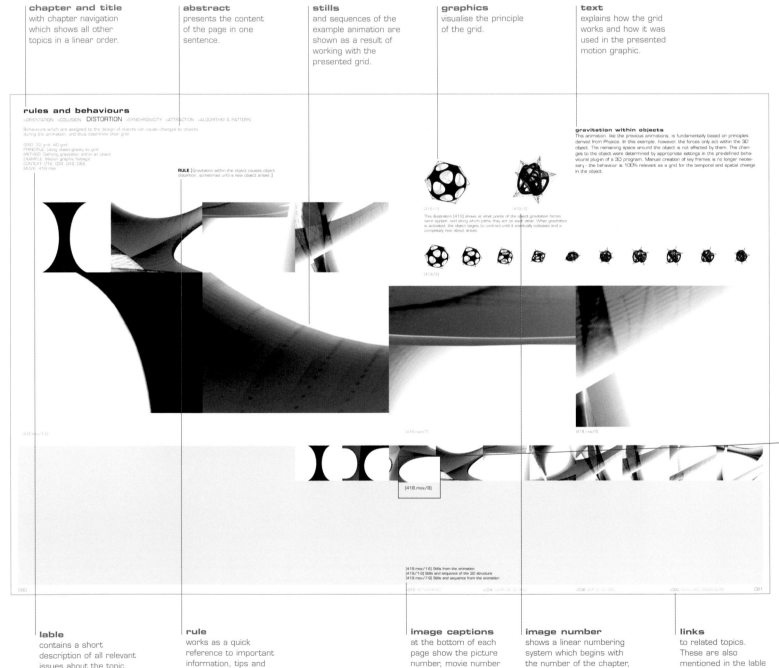

rules and behaviours
>ORIENTATION >COLUSION   DISTORTION >SYNCHRONICITY >ATTRACTION >ALGORITHM & PATTERN

Behaviours which are assigned to the design of objects can cause changes to objects during the animation, and thus determine their grid.

GRID: 3D grid, 4D grid
PRINCIPLE: Using object gravity as grid
METHOD: Defining gravitation within an object
EXAMPLE: Motion graphic footage
CONTEXT: 016, 034, 042, 056
MOVIE: 418.mov

RULE [Gravitation within the object causes object distortion, sometimes until a new object arises.]

gravitation within objects
This animation, like the previous animations, is fundamentally based on principles derived from Physics. In this example, however, the forces only act within the 3D object. The remaining space around the object is not affected by them. The changes to the object were determined by appropriate settings in the pre-defined behavioural plug-in of a 3D program. Manual creation of key frames is no longer necessary - the behaviour is 100% relevant as a grid for the temporal and spatial change in the object.

[419/1]   [419/2]

This illustration [419] shows at what points of the object gravitation forces were applied, and along which paths they act on each other. When gravitation is activated, the object begins to contract until it eventually collapses and a completely new object arises.

[419/3]

[418.mov/1-6]   [418.mov/7]   [418.mov/8]

[418.mov/9]

[418.mov/1-6] Stills from the animation
[419/1-3] Stills and sequence of the 3D structure
[418.mov/7-9] Stills and sequence from the animation

lable
contains a short description of all relevant issues about the topic, like the type of grid, the design principle, related topics and movies.

rule
works as a quick reference to important information, tips and rules.

image captions
at the bottom of each page show the picture number, movie number and content.

image number
shows a linear numbering system which begins with the number of the chapter, for example, 419/2 for the 19th motif in chapter four, still or sequence 2.

links
to related topics. These are also mentioned in the lable info under context by page number.

chapter openers
the red screens visualise
the 8 chapters. One
click on it opens the
chapter and presents
the relevant movies
visualised by white
screens.

selected movie
the selected movie
comes to the front and
can be started with the
controls.

context navigation
offers the option to select
movies by related
contexts.

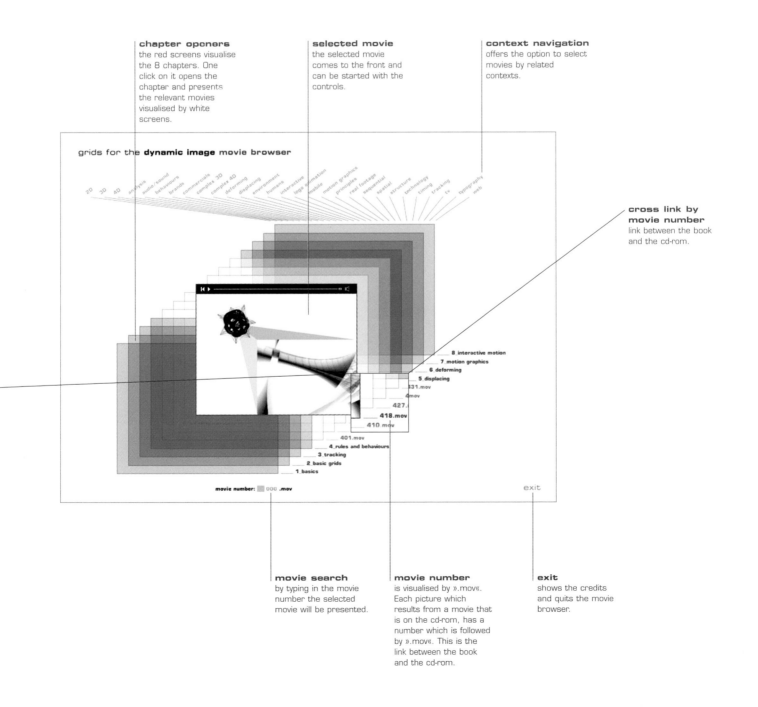

grids for the **dynamic image** movie browser

**cross link by
movie number**
link between the book
and the cd-rom.

8_interactive motion
7_motion graphics
6_deforming
5_displacing
431.mov
4.mov
427.
418.mov
410.mov
401.mov
4_rules and behaviours
3_tracking
2_basic grids
1_basics

movie number: 000 .mov

exit

movie search
by typing in the movie
number the selected
movie will be presented.

movie number
is visualised by ».mov«.
Each picture which
results from a movie that
is on the cd-rom, has a
number which is followed
by ».mov«. This is the
link between the book
and the cd-rom.

exit
shows the credits
and quits the movie
browser.

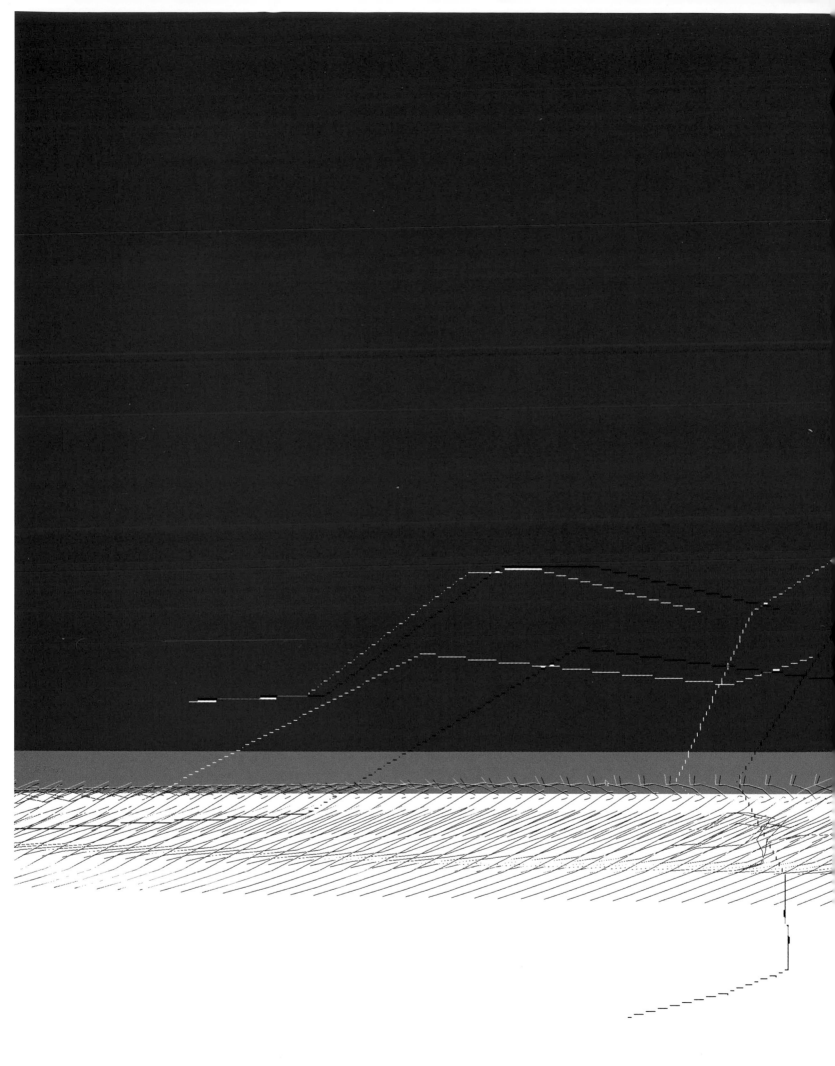

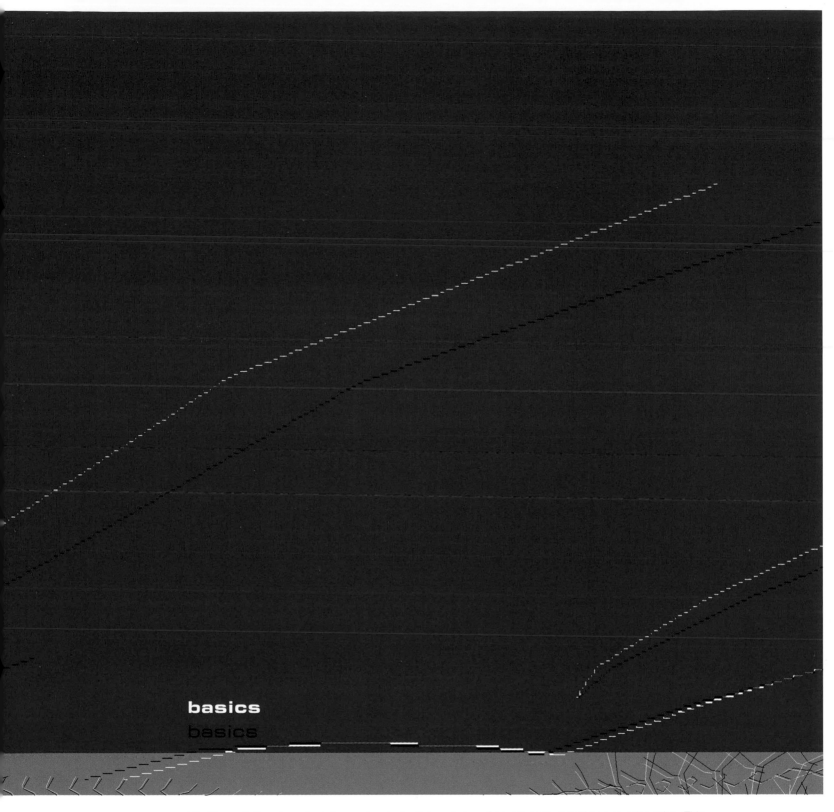

basics
basics

Working with time-based media requires in-depth knowledge of countless technical and creative rules. This relates to perception psychology factors and formal and structural aspects of the design of sequences as well as technical factors and the associated general conditions involved in output. The selection of the output medium can have a strong influence on the structural and design concept of the work. Even in pre-production it is often necessary to take the screen formats or technical formats into account in order to achieve best possible end results.

A knowledge of all technical, medium-related and design-oriented conditions and their properties can be impulse as well as basis for new creative solutions. Creative consideration of these phenomena can be found throughout this book.

basics

FORMATS >PIXELS & DISPLAYS >INTERLACING & FRAME RATES >NETWORKING >DRAMATURGY >TYPE & LEGIBILITY

Television standards define fixed values for frame rates, screen sizes or the aspect ratio of the output

RELATED GRID: 2D grid
FACTS: Relation between frame rates, screen size and aspect ratio
EXAMPLE: Overview of a few formats and resolutions
CONTEXT: 008, 012, 014, 026
MOVIE: –

Cellphone (Phones, I-Mode) TV HDTV
PDA (Handhelds, Mobile Devices) VGA (Computer Display, Data Projector, LED-Walls)

Cellphone 96x64
Cellphone 101x80
Cellphone 120x130
PDA 240x160
Cellphone 640x200
Cellphone 176x208
PDA 640x240
PDA 240x320
TV-NTSC 640x480
TV-NTSC D1 Squarepixel 720x540
TV-PAL D1 Squarepixel 768x576
VGA 800x600
HDTV 1280x720
VGA 1024x768
VGA 1280x1024
HDTV 1920x1080
VGA 1600x1200 VGA 1920x1200
VGA 2240x1400
Film-2K 2048x1536

[101]

formats and standards

In view of the fact that the area of moving image design has spread to numerous broadcast media such as the Internet and mobile terminal devices over recent years, there are a large number of formats and areas of technology which offer a field for design work. This ranges from displays for mobile phones to the high resolution of cinema films. The decisive factors for the output quality of animations include the size of the screen format, the data transmission method, the number of frames per second with which an animation is produced, the frame rate with which it is replayed and the output technology itself. Some technical formats result directly from the screen format. This applies, for example, to the most used television formats, NTSC and PAL.

Selecting the output format sometimes automatically defines the screen aspect ratio, because the definition of the format includes, for example, the number of lines transmitted per image, and this in turn, in conjunction with the pixels used, determines the screen format. For various standards there is therefore a direct correlation between the output format, the screen size and the frame rate. Therefore, the output format should already be taken into account when the moving image sequences are created so that the number of frames per second of the movie match with the number of frames the output media is broadcasting. For example, NTSC is replayed with 29.97 frames per second (fps) and PAL with 25 fps.

Film

|2500 |2600 |2700 |2800

Film-D16 2880x1536 ◢

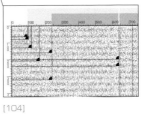

Cellphone 96x64
Cellphone 120x130
PDA 240x160
Cellphone 640x200 ◢
Cellphone 176x208
PDA 640x240 ◢
PDA 240x320 ◢
TV-NTSC 640x480 ◢

[103]

FORMAT*	RESOLUTION*	
Cellphone	96 x 64	Pixel
Cellphone	101 x 80	Pixel
Cellphone	120 x 130	Pixel
Cellphone	176 x 208	Pixel
PDA	240 x 160	Pixel
PDA	240 x 320	Pixel
Cellphone	640 x 200	Pixel
PDA	640 x 240	Pixel
TV-NTSC	640 x 480	Pixel
TV-NTSC D1 Squarepixel	720 x 540	Pixel
TV-PAL D1 Squarepixel	768 x 576	Pixel
VGA	800 x 600	Pixel
HDTV	1280 x 720	Pixel
VGA	1024 x 768	Pixel
VGA	1280 x 1024	Pixel
HDTV	1920 x 1080	Pixel
VGA	1600 x 1200	Pixel
VGA	1920 x 1200	Pixel
VGA	2240 x 1400	Pixel
Film-2K	2048 x 1536	Pixel
Film-D16	2880 x 1536	Pixel

*some formats and resolutions

[102]

[104]

Mobile phones
Today there are numerous screen formats for mobile devices such as mobile phones and handheld PCs. These formats not only differ in size, the screens often have device-specific aspect ratios.

NTSC (National Television Committee)
This format is used in the USA and Asia. It is adapted to the American electricity supply network (60 Hz). NTSC is displayed with a frame rate of 29.97 and a format of 640x480 pixels, which is built up of 480 visible lines out of a total of 525 scanning lines.

PAL (Phase Alternation Line)
The PAL format was developed in Germany and is optimised for the European electricity network (50 Hz). It is transmitted with a frame rate of 25 images per second and a format of 768x576 pixels, which is built up of 576 visible lines out of a total of 625 scanning lines.

basics

>FORMATS PIXELS & DISPLAYS >INTERLACING & FRAME RATES >NETWORKING >DRAMATURGY >TYPE & LEGIBILITY

In addition to square pixels there are also rectangular pixels which are used in some television standards
The picture quality and resolution of moving image sequences also depend on the output technology

RELATED GRID: 2D grid
FACTS: Pixels aspect ratio, output technology
EXAMPLE: Various pixel formats, display technologies
CONTEXT: 008, 010, 014, 022
MOVIE: 107.mov

INFO [In the format D1 NTSC the pixels have an aspect ratio of 0.9:1, (11/10), so they are slightly higher than wide, whereas the pixels in the PAL format (54/59) are slightly wider than high.]

[105/1]

Square pixels – While being displayed on a computer screen this circle remains a circle. This can be seen by the anti-aliasing reproduction (vertical and horizontal is consistent).

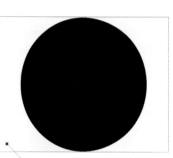

[105/2]

Applying high-format D1 NTSC pixels to the motif, the circle is clearly distorted to form an oval while watching it on a computer screen with square pixels. It is slightly wider than it is high. The height of the pixels has been distorted to the square format of the computer pixel – i.e. vertically »squeezed«.

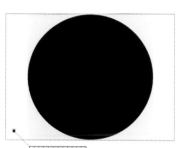

[105/3]

D1 NTSC pixels on a TV screen – The correct output device (TV screen) displays the D1 NTSC pixel motif in its original shape.

[106/1]

Square pixels – While being displayed on a computer screen this circle remains a circle. Which can be seen by the anti-aliasing reproduction (vertical and horizontal is consistent).

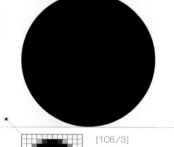

[106/2]

Applying horizontal-format PAL pixels to the motif and viewing it on a computer monitor, which displays square pixels, the circle is clearly distorted to form an oval which is slightly higher than it is wide. The width of the pixels has been distorted to the square format of the computer pixel – i.e. horizontally »squeezed«.

[106/3]

PAL pixels on a TV screen – The correct output device (TV screen) displays the PAL pixel motif in its original shape.

pixels

Each picture on a screen is made up of a large number of individual dots or pixels. A common aspect of all formats is the smallest unit - the dot, picture element or pixel. Depending on each output device, this is differently generated or technically composed. The size of a pixel is determined by the number of dots per inch (dpi), e.g. 72 dpi or 96 dpi, and by the aspect ratio of the pixel, e.g. 1:1, 0.9:1 etc.
The higher the resolution, the smaller the individual pixel.

In addition to square pixels there are also rectangular pixels which are used in some television standards. In addition to the aspect ratio of the sequence (e.g. 4:3 or 16:9), the aspect ratio of the individual pixels that a picture is made up of must also be taken into account. Not all moving image sequences are made up of square pixels. There are formats, such as D1 NTSC or PAL video, which are displayed with rectangular pixels, so-called »non-square pixels«. This might cause distorted displayed pictures while watching them for example on a computer screen.

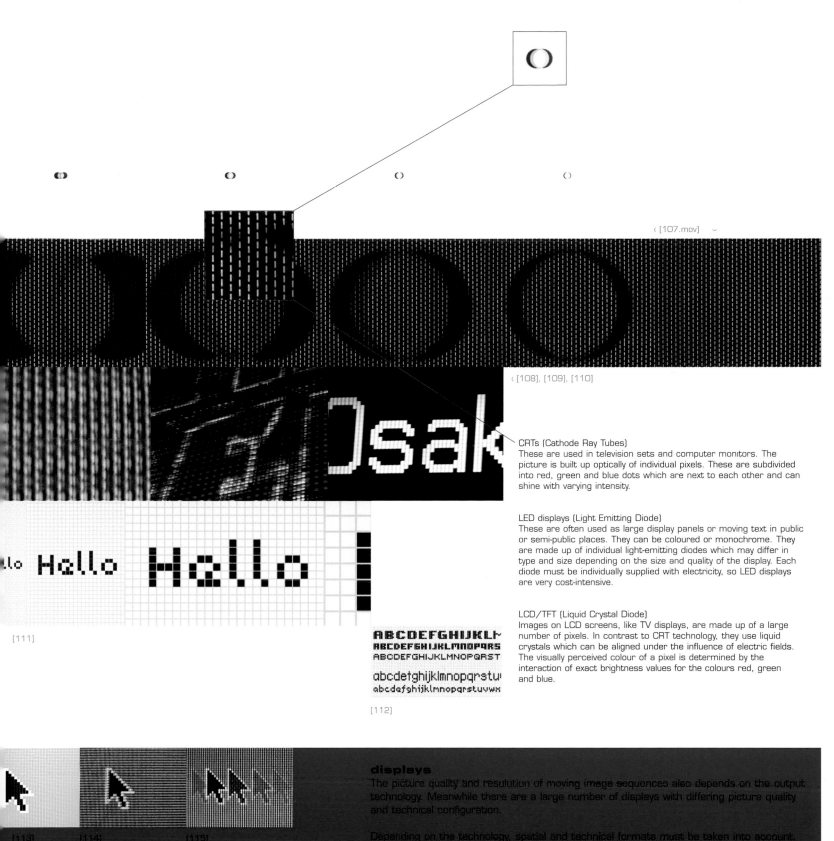

⟨ [107.mov]   ⌄

⟨ [108], [109], [110]

CRTs (Cathode Ray Tubes)
These are used in television sets and computer monitors. The picture is built up optically of individual pixels. These are subdivided into red, green and blue dots which are next to each other and can shine with varying intensity.

LED displays (Light Emitting Diode)
These are often used as large display panels or moving text in public or semi-public places. They can be coloured or monochrome. They are made up of individual light-emitting diodes which may differ in type and size depending on the size and quality of the display. Each diode must be individually supplied with electricity, so LED displays are very cost-intensive.

LCD/TFT (Liquid Crystal Diode)
Images on LCD screens, like TV displays, are made up of a large number of pixels. In contrast to CRT technology, they use liquid crystals which can be aligned under the influence of electric fields. The visually perceived colour of a pixel is determined by the interaction of exact brightness values for the colours red, green and blue.

[111]

[112]

displays
The picture quality and resolution of moving image sequences also depends on the output technology. Meanwhile there are a large number of displays with differing picture quality and technical configuration.

Depending on the technology, spatial and technical formats must be taken into account. Usually there is a close connection between the technical characteristics of displays, the frame rate, the aspect ratio and finally the visual quality. The choice of projection technology affects the picture quality and its output quality. Depending on the display, both the design and the production technology should be adapted to the corresponding output format.

[113]   [114]   [115]

[105/1] Pixel display on a computer monitor
[105/2] Non-square pixel display (NTSC) on a computer
[105/3] Non-square pixel display (NTSC) on a TV
[106/1] Pixel display on a computer monitor
[106/2] Non-square pixel display (PAL) on a computer
[106/3] Non-square pixel display (PAL) on a TV
[107.mov] Sequence display on a TV monitor
[108] TV screen
[109–10] LED/OLED
[111] Screen font 5 px
[112] Screen font with different letter spacing, size and style
[113] Display of a cursor in the pixel grid
[114] Display on a TFT screen
[115] Display on a CRT screen

basics

Television standards transmit the picture signals in the form of fields. By this means, twice as many fields as whole pictures can be transmitted
Unsynchronised output of television pictures on computer monitors causes line flickering

RELATED GRID: 2D grid
FACTS: Field rendering, line flickering
EXAMPLE: Field rendering, correlation of frame rate and hertz frequency of output media
CONTEXT: 008, 010, 012, 022
MOVIES: 117.mov, 121.mov

[116]

[118]

[117.mov/1]

TIP [Whether footage is produced with or without interlacing should always be decided on the basis of the existing material or the output medium. For example, if typography is rendered on a non-interlaced film, interlacing would change the whole aesthetic effect. Conversely, a non-interlaced typographic animation on interlaced footage would appear very ragged and would also impair the effect.]

[117.mov/2]

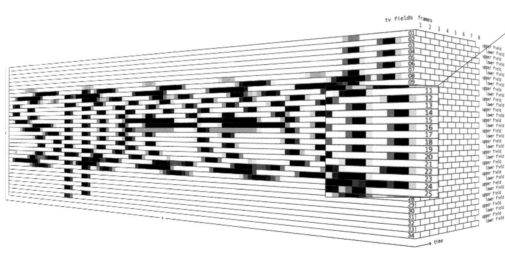

This rendering shows the word »speed« which is moving from right to left. The two fields which are transmitted one after the other are visible. In each field, only every second line is shown. The lines of the two fields are interlaced with each other, so that the inertia of the eye produces the impression of a complete television picture.

The time axis shows the sequence of the fields one after another.

[119]

television standards - interlacing

Television standards transmit the picture signals in the form of fields. By this means, twice as many fields as whole pictures can be transmitted.
By contrast with computer monitors, which display whole images, all television formats operate with fields. Each field contains only every second line. For transmission, the so-called interlacing method is used. In the NTSC standard 60 fields are transmitted per second, and in PAL standard 50 fields are transmitted per second.

Depending on the television standard (e.g. NTSC, PAL etc.), the total number of lines transmitted to generate the image (e.g. 525 for NTSC and 625 for PAL) are broken down into two fields of 262.5 (NTSC) or 312.5 lines (PAL) respectively. The two fields are transmitted one after the other with a slight offset so that they again make up one picture in the eyes of the viewer. The lines of the two fields are interlaced with each other, so that the inertia of the eye produces the impression of a complete television picture.

When sequences are produced for television, field rendering enables the images to be broken down into fields in the sequence rendering stage. To this end, it is possible to define the line that is to be transmitted first (upper or lower field). Especially in moving image sequences, the selection of the first field to be transmitted plays a major role. It is the crucial factor that determines whether the animation looks smooth or not. The process of field rendering or interlacing means that the number of pictures transmitted appears to be twice as high (although they are in fact only fields or half images), and this creates a much smoother representation of movement on the screen.

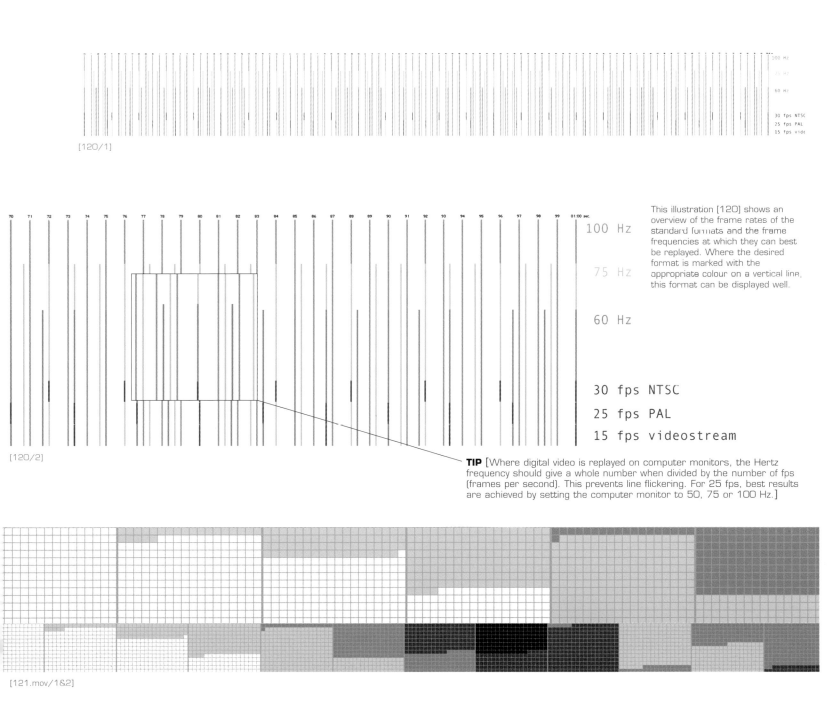

[120/1]

[70 71 72 73 74 75 76 77 78 79 80 81 82 83 84 85 86 87 88 89 90 91 92 93 94 95 96 97 98 99 01:00 sec.]

100 Hz

75 Hz

60 Hz

30 fps NTSC

25 fps PAL

15 fps videostream

[120/2]

This illustration [120] shows an overview of the frame rates of the standard formats and the frame frequencies at which they can best be replayed. Where the desired format is marked with the appropriate colour on a vertical line, this format can be displayed well.

TIP [Where digital video is replayed on computer monitors, the Hertz frequency should give a whole number when divided by the number of fps (frames per second). This prevents line flickering. For 25 fps, best results are achieved by setting the computer monitor to 50, 75 or 100 Hz.]

[121.mov/1&2]

To achieve optimum results in the output of moving image sequences, it is first of all necessary to synchronise the number of images per second in the animation (fps) with the number of images prescribed or offered by the replay format. Especially the television formats NTSC and PAL are bound by fixed fps values. Thus, PAL is displayed on computer monitors with 25 fps and NTSC with 29.97 fps.

If the frame rate does not match the moving image resolution (i.e. if the images per second in the animation do not match the number of images that can be output), it can lead to line flickering. This most frequently happens on computer monitors because they offer numerous frame frequency settings.

Line flickering occurs if the replay device offers a Hertz frequency which does not give a whole number when divided by the number of frames per second in which the animation was created. With a Hertz frequency of 25, if the replay device is properly calibrated, the time for the display of each frame is exactly 1/25 second. If the Hertz frequency is 50, each image in a 25 fps animation can be shown twice within the second. If NTSC is used and the rendering is only 29.97 fps, line flickering occurs at 25 Hz, and also at 50 Hz, 75 Hz and 100 Hz. NTSC never conforms with the Hertz frequency of a monitor because of the interpolation of 29.97 fps to 30 fps, so line flickering always occurs.

[116] 2D diagram of a field rendering, slow animation
[117.mov/1] Still of a TV screen with visible fields
[117.mov/2] Cut-out from TV still
[118] 2D diagram of a field rendering, fast animation
[119] 3D diagram of a field rendering
[120/1] Overview of frame frequency/fps
[120/2] Overview of matching frame frequency/fps
[121.mov/1] Image build-up from top left to bottom right
[121.mov/2] Image build-up becomes increasingly fast

basics

Working with time-based media requires networked and non-linear structures in the organisation and construction of animations

RELATED GRID: 4D grid
FACTS: Non-linear structures, networking
EXAMPLE: Non-linear software interfaces
CONTEXT: 046, 066, 088, 124, 164
MOVIE: –

This sample shows an interface of a DVD authoring tool. The non-linear structure shows the user which relationships between the individual files he or she has already created.

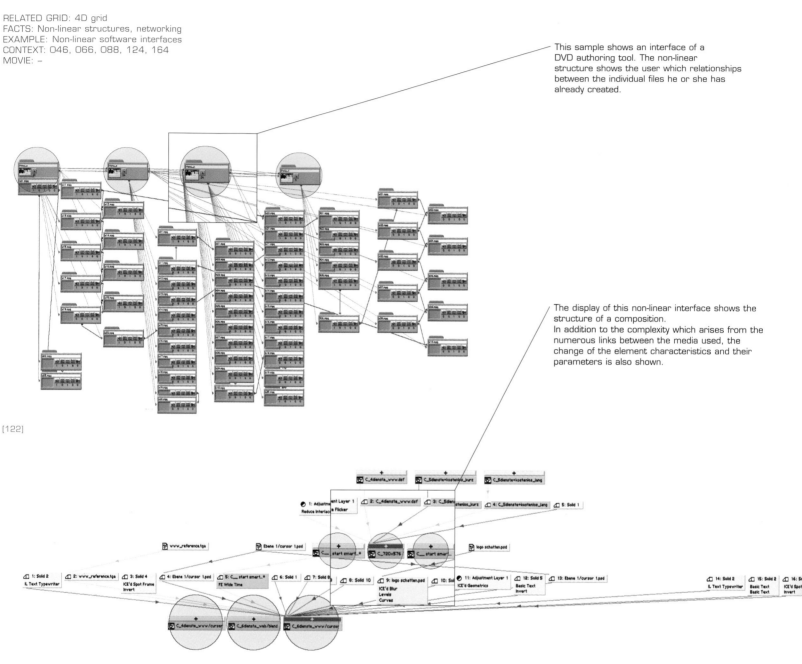

[122]

The display of this non-linear interface shows the structure of a composition.
In addition to the complexity which arises from the numerous links between the media used, the change of the element characteristics and their parameters is also shown.

[123]

networking

Graphical elements are often interrelated not only in their visual characteristics but also in their structure. This is a central aspect of the design of motion graphics because other parameters of graphical change can be defined in addition to the creation of links and interrelationships between graphical elements. The design not only defines that two elements are in relation to each other; it also defines in what way the elements are related. Thus, the link itself can also be assigned to a set of rules or laws.

These interdependent relationships and the ability to design the links between the graphical and film elements are now taken into account by numerous programs. Thus, a number of tools have been developed to give the user the possibility of directly editing the structure he or she has already created by displaying it.

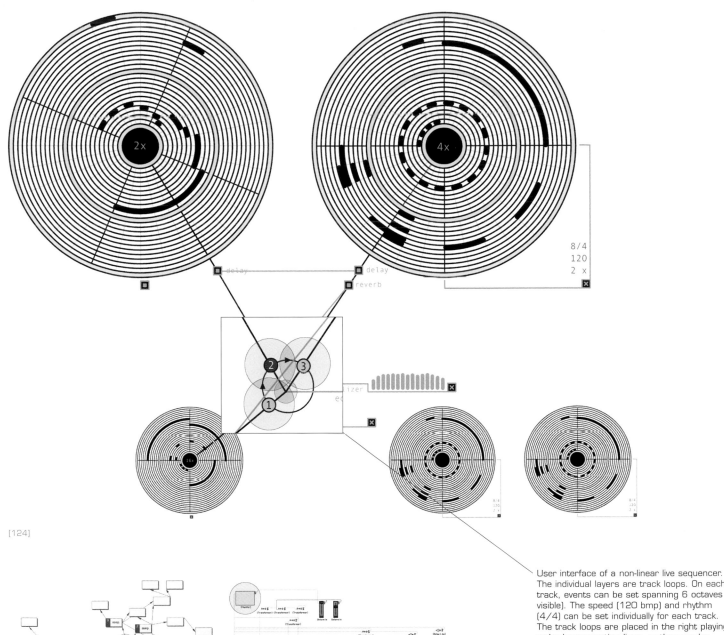

[124]

User interface of a non-linear live sequencer. The individual layers are track loops. On each track, events can be set spanning 6 octaves (2 visible). The speed (120 bmp) and rhythm (4/4) can be set individually for each track. The track loops are placed in the right playing order by connecting lines, or they can be manipulated live from the console (red marking). Effects such as delay and echo are dragged directly on to the appropriate patch lines.

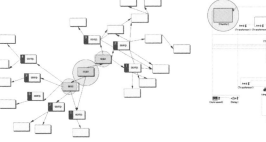

[125]

[126]

In addition to the area of compositing, which is often portrayed as a time-based function, many programs also offer the possibility of viewing self-created links and the structure of the content. This usually includes the ability to change the links and relationships and to manipulate the parameters in other ways. Especially with complex sequences, these features simplify organisation and orientation in compositions that have already been created.

Especially moving image editing and authoring programs offer the option of combination and allocation to groups, a modular principle that ensures a way of working that is well organised and nevertheless creative. This, for example, enables layers to be combined into compositions. Just as properties are »inherited« in object-oriented programming, this function facilitates object-oriented, layer-oriented and group-oriented design (compositions).

[122] Non-linear interface of a DVD authoring tool
[123] Non-linear structure of a composition
[124] User interface of a non-linear live sequencer
[125] Interface of a mind-mapping tool
[126] Interface of a midi sequencer

basics

The success of an exciting dramaturgy is decisively affected by the interaction of the individual graphics and
media (layers) and the balance between design, movement and timing

RELATED GRID: 4D grid
FACTS: Balance between design, movement and timing
EXAMPLE: Visualisation of dramaturgy of an effect of a layer
CONTEXT: 008, 038, 046, 066, 088, 106, 124
MOVIE: 127.mov

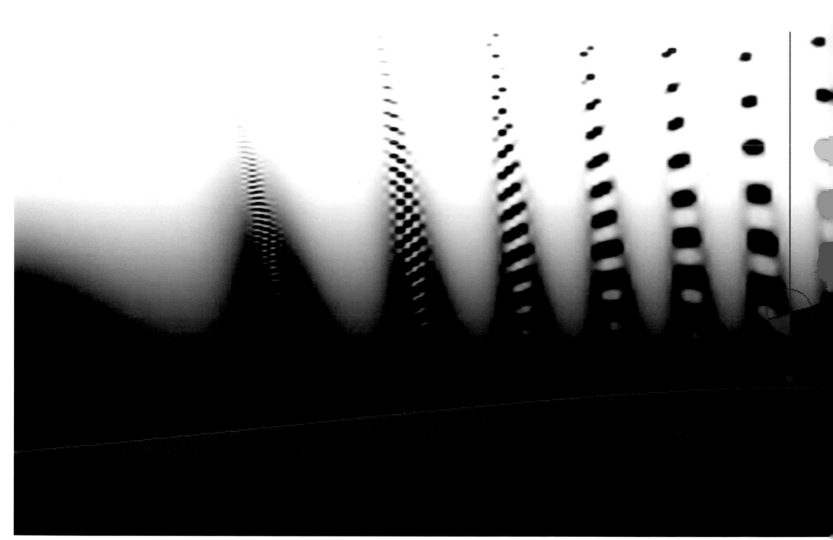

[127.mov/1]

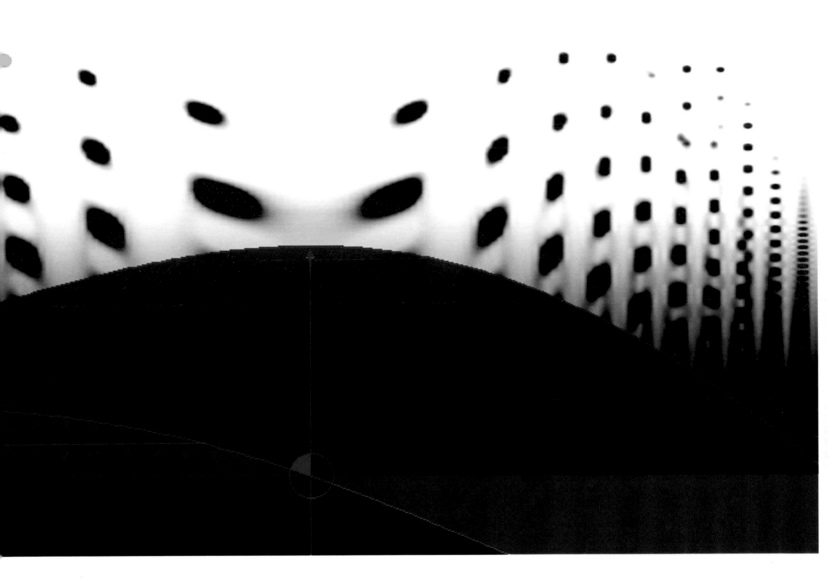

dramaturgy

When designing moving image sequences it is especially important to create a good dramaturgy. Due to their dynamic character, animations have the potential to exercise strong control over the attention of the viewer. It is possible to create very exciting and emotionally gripping animations, but equally possible to create boring animations. The art, depending on the goal of the project, is to create a virtuoso relationship between rest and movement, slow and fast.

The success of an exciting dramaturgy is decisively affected by the interaction of the individual graphics and media (layers) and the balance between design, movement and timing. This should always be created individually by the designer on the basis of his or her discretion and experience. There are no rules for the systematic control of audience attention or the creation of a reliable dramaturgy. Each animation has different communication goals, media, graphical elements and intentions, so it is next to impossible to create any general rules. It is important to grasp the complex interaction of object, form, movement and timing and then to shape this interaction as the designer wishes, and thus to create the desired dramaturgy.

basics

The creation of dramaturgy in motion graphics depends on the precise coordination of the design, the movement and the change of element parameters

RELATED GRID: 4D grid
PRINCIPLE: Measure of change and intensity of effects
METHOD: Coordination of graphical elements/layers
EXAMPLE: Visualisation of the dramaturgy of various effects of graphic elements
CONTEXT: 008, 038, 046, 066, 088, 106, 124
MOVIE: 127.mov

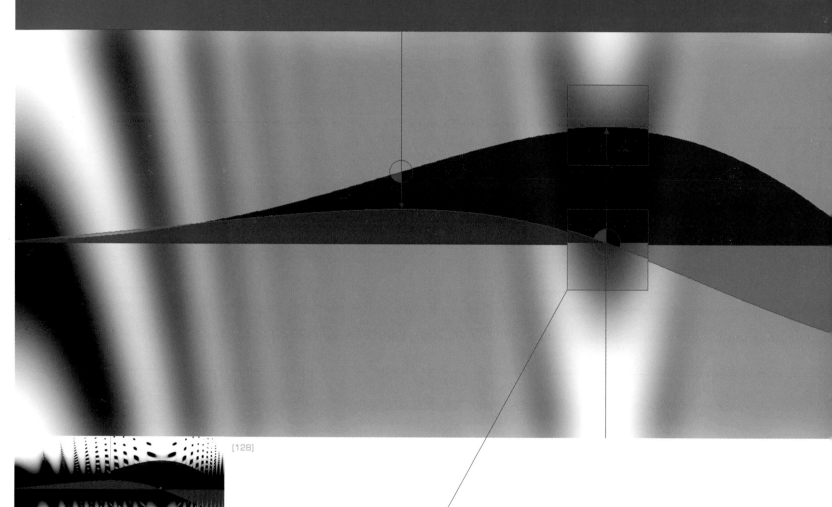

[128]

[127.mov/2]

INFO [These illustrations show first of all the parameter changes of the properties of elements/layers or the overlaying filters (black) and secondly the intensity of these changes over time (red). If much changes in a short time, the red curve is seen to rise. The vertical positioning of the individual points on the graphs shows the relative change of the value in relation to one frame before and one frame after the current frame.]

dramaturgy

To create dramaturgically interesting animations, all parameter changes of the elements designed or used should be precisely geared to match each other. This means that the changes of the graphical elements over time must be matched in relation to themselves and the other elements. Usually changes not only take place in one parameter of an object (e.g. the size by scaling) but in several parameters (e.g. size and brightness), so the balance between the changes in the individual objects is just as necessary as the interaction between all elements used and their changes over time.

[128] Illustration of a dramaturgy curve
[127.mov/2] Illustration of a dramaturgy curve
[129–32] Modification (black) and dynamics (red) of three graphical elements/layers
[133] Dramaturgy, notation of a frequency
[134] Extract of the notation

⟨ [129]

⟨ [130]

⟨ [131]

⟨ [132]

Dramaturgies are often designed by making a change in the individual element directly or indirectly dependent on other elements. In simple animations, for instance, this can mean that a new element appears when another disappears, and so on. But it can also mean that parameter changes in certain elements have an effect on the parameters of other elements (more on this in the chapter on Tracking -> 046).

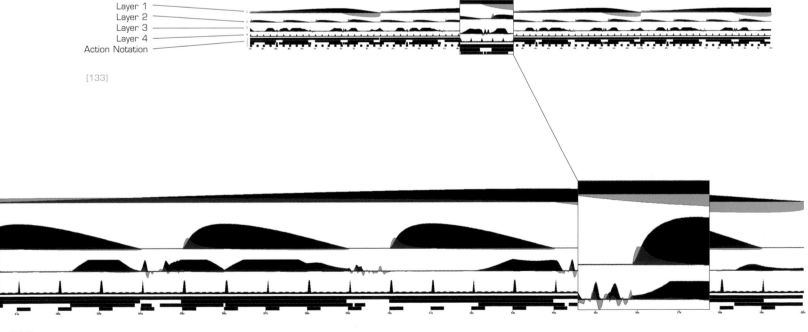

Layer 1
Layer 2
Layer 3
Layer 4
Action Notation

[133]

[134]

basics

The legibility of typography on the screen is determined by numerous factors, such as the type size, animation speed and duration of presence. Processes such as easing are useful means of extending the duration of the legible zone of the typography

RELATED GRID: 4D grid
PRINCIPLE: Using easing to expand legibility of moving typography
METHOD: Temporal change of speed
EXAMPLE: Typographic animation
CONTEXT: 008, 018, 038, 058, 090,124
MOVIES: 135.mov, 138.mov

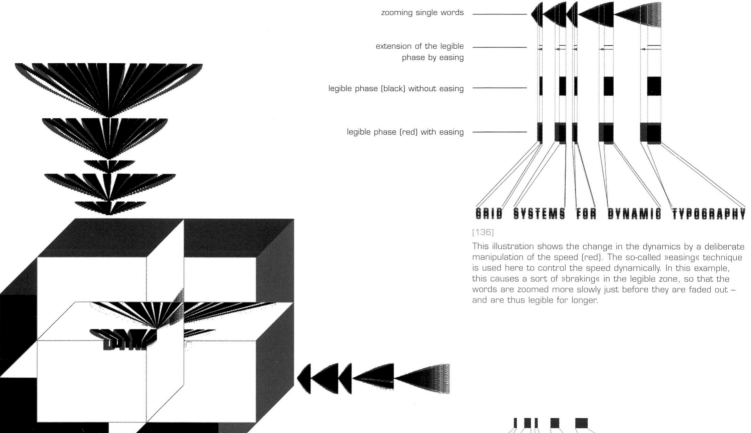

zooming single words

extension of the legible
phase by easing

legible phase (black) without easing

legible phase (red) with easing

[136]

This illustration shows the change in the dynamics by a deliberate manipulation of the speed (red). The so-called »easing« technique is used here to control the speed dynamically. In this example, this causes a sort of »braking« in the legible zone, so that the words are zoomed more slowly just before they are faded out – and are thus legible for longer.

[137]

[135.mov]

The linear zoom [135.mov] is portrayed in the x, y, and z axis by an analytical program. The change in the size of the individual words is visible. The height of the cone shows the display duration for each word. As the words are zoomed from 0% to 100%, the legible zone of the type is only visible for a short time. It only occurs in the last quarter of the zoom when the type is larger than 14 point. How long the legible phase lasts depends in turn on the type size and the speed of the animation.

legibility

The legibility of type in animations depends on various factors. For example, the type size, type of animation and speed play an important role, as does the duration for which the typography is visible in the scene. As a rule it must always be ensured that the type is legible in spite of the movement and design.

First of all, an appropriate type size must be selected. This depends on the medium on which the animation is to be displayed. Text on a computer, for example, can be legible at a size of 5 pixels, but type sizes of at least 14–20 point are necessary for television productions.

As typography is frequently superimposed or animated, a decisive factor for the legibility of animated type is the time for which it is visible on the screen. Allowance must be made for the fact that short words can be read faster than long words. The length of time words are displayed on the screen must therefore be adapted to the length of the words. The number of syllables in a word can be used as a guide, so that a second can be used for one syllable.

[138.mov/2]

[138.mov/3]

[138.mov/1]

RULE [The legibility time for animated typography is measured by the length of the words or the number of syllables. A second for each syllable should be designated in the legibility zone.]

[139]

GRID SYSTEMS FOR DYNAMIC TYPOGRAPHY

[140]

GRID SYSTEMS FOR DYNAMIC TYPOGRAPHY

[141]

This illustration shows an analysis of an animation in which each word »Grid systems for dynamic typography« is zoomed in continuously.

It becomes clear that short words are visible less long than long words.

This illustration shows an analysis of an animation in which each word »Grid systems for dynamic typography« is zoomed in with the use of »easing«.

Easing – the manipulation of the speed of a layer at single points – is a common technique to create dramatic effects and a smoother flow of the animation. It is used in text animation to enhance legibility, because the readable zone is visible for a longer time.

This illustration shows an analysis of an animation in which each word »Grid systems for dynamic typography« is faded in consecutively, then abruptly faded out again.

It can clearly be seen that the words »grids« and »for« are on the screen for a shorter time than the other words, as it requires less time to read them.

But if the type is not just superimposed and faded out, but also animated, the legible phase of the text must also be considered. This is especially relevant for animated type which changes its size on the screen, i.e. scaled type. It may only be legible for a short phase of the animation – the phase when the type has reached a legible size. This phase can be extended by using a technique known as »easing«. In this process, the temporary speed of a graphical element is changed at different points within an animation: it is accelerated or decelerated at specific points in the animation. This can produce a dramatic effect and a more »flowing« appearance of the animations.

»Easing« is often used in typographic animation to prolong the legible phase of the type. Depending on the length of time a word is animated, the legible zone may be shorter or longer. This zone depends on the continuity of the speed in the animation. If the text is animated at an even speed, the legible phase is only legible for a short part of the animation period, depending on the type size and the speed of the animation.

To enhance legibility and help viewers to grasp the words, the speed can be changed precisely, i.e. slowed down, in certain parts of the animation. In this way, the type will move more quickly at the start of the zoom than at the end, when the animation speed is slowed down as it is only there that the type has reached its legible size.

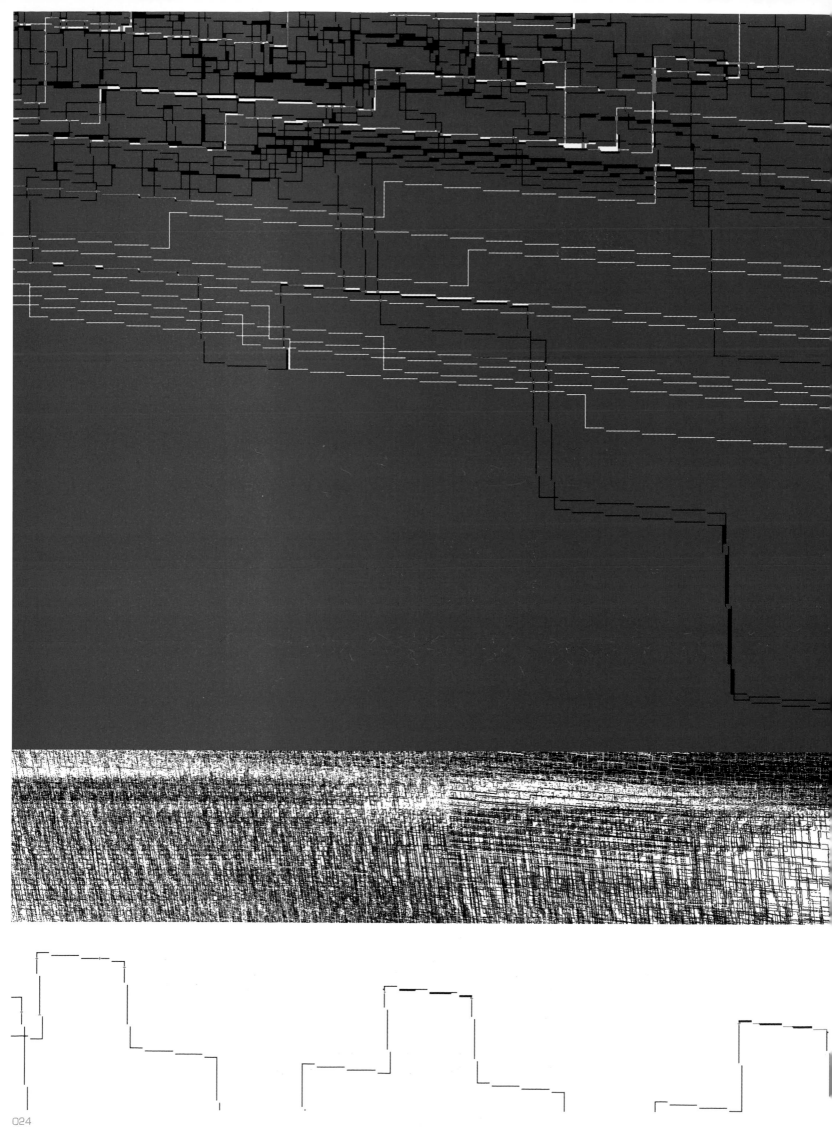

basic grids
basic grids

Grids are necessary to position design features, media, and contents such as images, texts and video, etc. They have the function of determining over a longer period the interaction and positioning of media contents. But what does »positioning« mean when we are talking about animation and interactive applications? This no longer involves placing static items on the page of a book or magazine, and choosing a layout. Rather than just arranging things on a flat surface it is also necessary to determine the constellation of the elements in space, and their behaviour over time.

The positioning on the surface, in space and time can be defined by grids. There are three types of basic grids that we call 2D, 3D and 4D grids. A 2D grid determines the behaviour on a flat surface, a 3D grid determines the behaviour in space and a 4D grid determines the behaviour in time.

Grids for time-based media are often built by determining a set of rules. During the animation they steer the elements or their behaviour in the desired way. Every type of grid (2D, 3D, 4D) might contain a certain part of a different grid. For example, a 3D grid might contain a 4D grid. This means that a 3D grid can also determine the behaviour over time. We define a grid as 2D, 3D and 4D, if the essential impact is determined by the behaviour in the corresponding dimension. Depending on the type of animation there is always a dominant grid.

Subsequently we will initially introduce the different categories of grids. In other chapters we will discuss principles and methods for the creation and usage of grids and sets of rules.

basic grids

2D GRIDS > 3D GRIDS > 4D GRIDS

2D grids are used for screen design and animations with a low level of complexity.

GRID: Simple 2D grid
PRINCIPLE: Using simple 2D grids to determine proportions on a surface
METHOD: Creating zones and units
EXAMPLE: Screen grids for computers and mobiles
CONTEXT: 012, 022, 029, 186
MOVIE: 2DS.mov

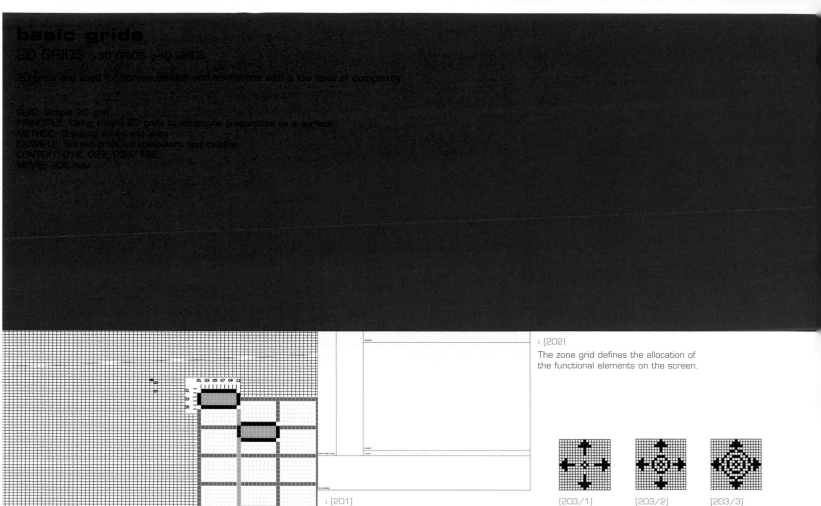

< [202]
The zone grid defines the allocation of the functional elements on the screen.

[203/1]   [203/2]   [203/3]

< [201]
The screen grid ensures that all components of the interface are positioned in the step size of the smallest grid unit.

2D screen grid
A 2D grid can determine, as in print applications, the x and y coordinates on the screen for various elements such as movies or integrated animations. In screen design for interactive applications, a zoning plan is first produced which integrates the functional units on the screen. The zones are then assigned their own appropriate sub-grids.

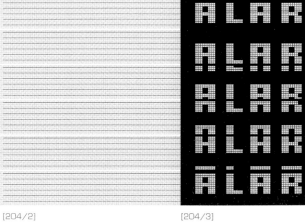

[204/1]   [204/2]   [204/3]

simple 2D grid
A 2D grid determines the positioning and movement in two-dimensions of layout elements, media and contents such as images, text, sound and video, etc. A 2D grid is of lower complexity, but may often determine not only the positioning and movement of objects, but also their timing – depending on whether the grid is intended for animations or for interactive applications. For the latter, functional zones will usually be formed to which specific media such as text or video will be assigned. In animation, the grid generally determines the dramaturgy, which is very similar in a time-based design to print design, where the tension is also determined by the features of the grid and their implementation.

[204/4]

+ 3 Pixel

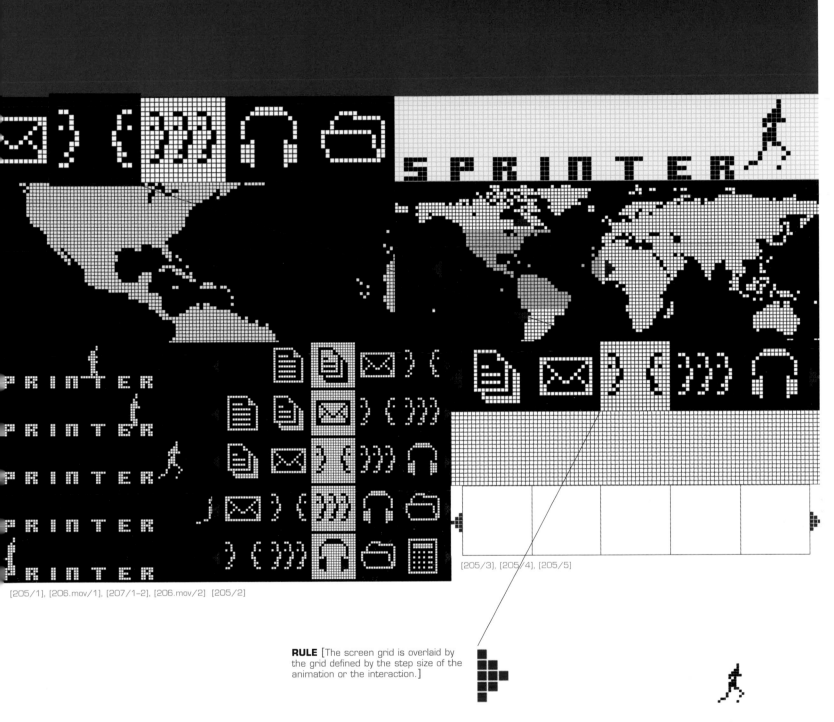

[205/1], [206.mov/1], [207/1-2], [206.mov/2] [205/2]

[205/3], [205/4], [205/5]

RULE [The screen grid is overlaid by the grid defined by the step size of the animation or the interaction.]

ticker-text

A very simple grid might involve a ticker-text moving continually from side to side on a screen or from top to bottom. Ticker-text is extremely effective, and in public spaces, on TV or on websites it often attracts attention due to the association with up-to-date messages, rather than the type of animation. But the speed at which the text moves is dictated by reading speed, which therefore determines the time grid.

Another very simple grid determines where and how one or more text or graphic elements move in two dimensions. The example [205] shows how every click of a button on a mobile phone moves an icon nearer towards the centre of the display. There is an overlap of the pixel grid and the functional grid, defining the length of the »steps« taken.

basic grids

2D GRIDS >3D GRIDS >4D GRIDS

Graphic elements which are used as a model for other elements can be
linked in the form of path or transformation grids

GRID: Complex 2D grid
PRINCIPLE: Using complex 2D grids to transform real footage
METHOD: Morphing and path animation
EXAMPLE: Eye and body morphing, typographic animation with paths
CONTEXT: 024, 046, 104, 114, 140, 150
MOVIE: –

This example shows how the transformation of the picture
material depends on the transformation of the grid. This
picture shows the grid and the picture without any link, the
grid is merely superimposed on the picture.

In the second picture, the first change is already visible.
The pupil has been increased from the inner circle to the
size of the outer circle of the grid. In the process, however,
not only the pupil itself has become bigger, which would
happen with simple scaling, but the area around the pupil,
almost the whole picture, has also been affected.

This is clearly seen in the third picture. The transformation
of the outer circle, including the shape of the star, has an
influence on the motif even outside the grid, as the
displaced parts of the image must now create a transition
between the changed form and the original form.

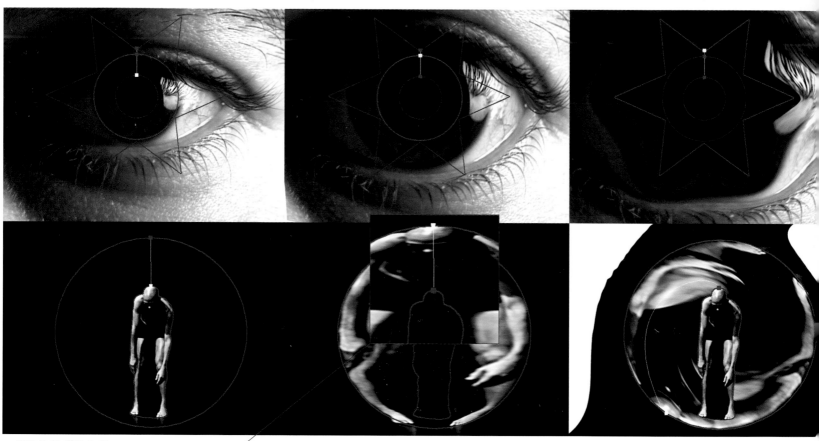

[208/1–3], [209/1–3]

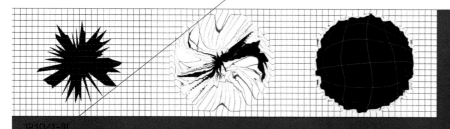

[210/1–3]

The second row of pictures shows the transformation of a motif from the outline of a human body
to a large circle. Such manipulations of graphical elements are often generated automatically by
the use of filters. But it is also possible to create these effects manually with self-created grids.
The third picture in the row shows another manipulation of the image. An anti-clockwise rotation
has been added. The picture shows both the original status and the end status of the
transformation. Here, too, the transformation has an affect even beyond the edges of the grid.

morphing

In motion graphics design, 2D grids are used not only to position the
elements, but also to determine their movement and coordinate the
movements of various elements, i.e. the timing. To this end a grid and its
format change over time, can be used as a basis for the transformation of
an illustration or a moving picture sequence. This process changes the
form of both the grid and the object. Many of the filters that exist today in
digital design are based on this principle. A simple shape which serves as
a grid is linked with the motif which is to be changed. If the grid is changed
within a defined period, the motif is also changed in the same way as the
grid. The grid itself can determine the form of the change.

TIP [The further the points of a path are from each other, the faster the graphical element will be, because the distance which must be overcome between two frames is greater.]

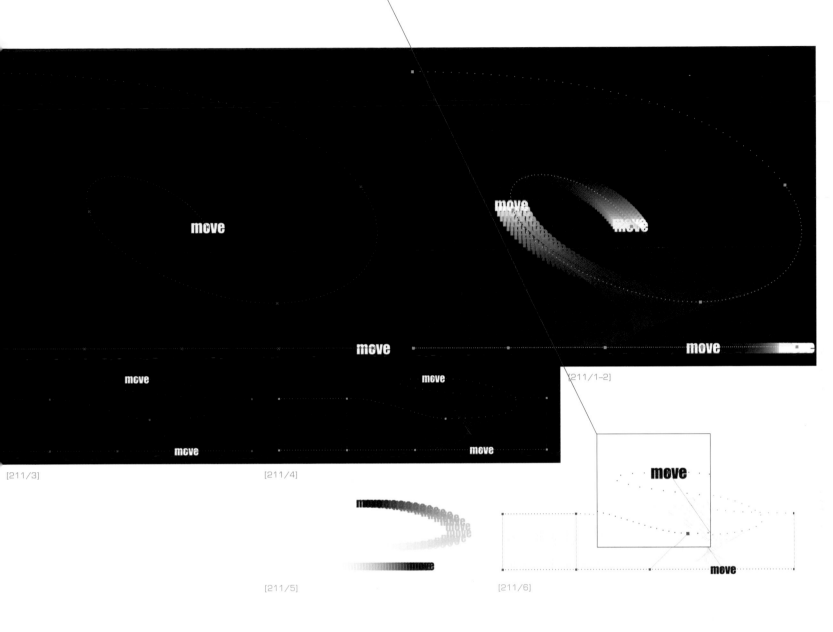

[211/3]

[211/4]

[211/1-2]

[211/5]

[211/6]

paths

A further possibility to work with 2D grids is to create a path. To do this, a path can be imported from other programs as a model or drawn directly in the program, or it is generated in real time in a sort of recording mode. Paths can be used as grids for placing in time and space, i.e. for the movement of graphical elements. With the movement that takes place within a certain period and in a certain zone on the screen, they also define the dynamics of an element. Like in the real world, there is a direct relationship between the path and the time needed to travel it. This relationship also determines the speed of the graphical element in its digital form. It can vary from frame to frame.

If a large distance is travelled in a short time, the speed is greater than if a short distance is travelled in a longer time. Most programs show the position of the object in each frame as a dot or cross on its path. The distance between these points indicates how fast the graphical element is in the respective positions. Most programs now offer the possibility of either moving the object by the appropriate frame or changing the sequence of the path. In both cases, this affects the sequence of the animation.

[208/1-3] Morphing outside a defined zone
[209/1-3] Morphing to another form
[210/1-3] Morphing within a defined zone
[211/1-6] Comparison of linear and dynamic animation paths

basic grids

Very simple 3D grids only create a virtual third dimension

GRID: Simple 3D grid
PRINCIPLE: Using simple 3D grids to create virtual layers
METHOD: Subdividing space into layers
EXAMPLE: Typographic animation
CONTEXT: 014, 022, 024, 124
MOVIE: –

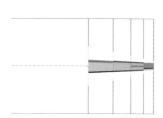

[212]

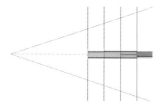

[213]

VIEW

[214]

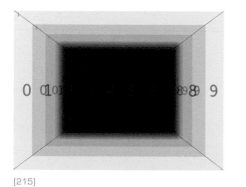

[215]

In a simple 3D grid the (simulated) space is subdivided into various virtual layers. Each layer represents in principle a 2D grid for this spatial segment, determining the movement and timing of the elements anchored there. The layers are lined up on the z axis and specify both the movement and the speed of the objects.

simple 3D grid

We distinguish between two types of 3D grid. Firstly, a grid can regulate the behaviour of an object in three dimensions in the same way as a 2D grid does on a surface. Alternatively, a grid may influence the space (e.g. by deformation) and thus affect the dynamics and the behaviour of the object, or even change its shape.

3D grids can have different characteristics. There is a 3D grid which assigns layers to the space and determines the movements of the object for each layer separately.

A complex 3D grid can take on the »effect« assigned to a space. In this case the 3D grid is used as a displacement for the objects and their paths.

[216]

RULE [To generate a spatial dimension, simple means such as type size, blur and speed can be used to create a parallactic display. The typography in the foreground is larger and moves faster than the typography in the background.]

Particularly when animations generate three-dimensional impressions but are not actually produced with 3D programs, it is very important to work with perception phenomena. These can be used to suggest depth and space. In this way it is possible to derive rules that can be very helpful in the creation of 3D grids.

If, as in this example, the desire is to create the impression that all lines of text move at the same pace, but at various distances from each other, it is imperative to exactly determine the timing of each individual layer.

[212] Real view of the levels of the z axis
[213] Simulated view of the levels of the z axis
[214] Levels of a 3D grid on the z axis
[215] Frontal view of a simple 3D grid
[216] Sequence of an animation with a three-dimensional effect

basic grids

>2D GRIDS 3D GRIDS >4D GRIDS

Simple 3D grids create a spatial orientation, like 2D grids on a surface

GRID: Simple 3D grid
PRINCIPLE: Using simple 3D grids to create order in space
METHOD: Transforming two-dimensional order into space, defining functional units
EXAMPLE: Virtual studio (TV) interface
CONTEXT: 024, 026, 126, 164
MOVIE: –

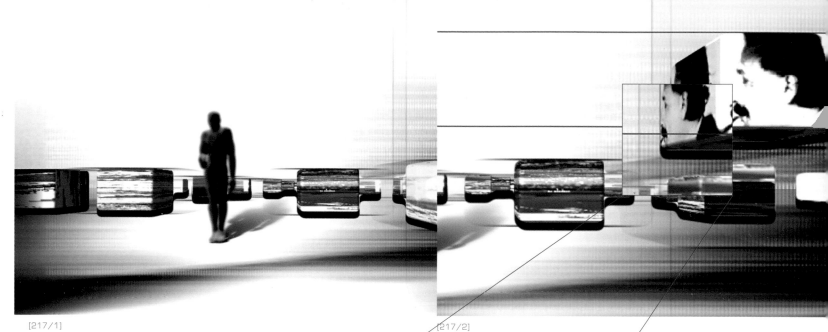

[217/1]　　　　　　　　　　　　　　　　　　　　　[217/2]

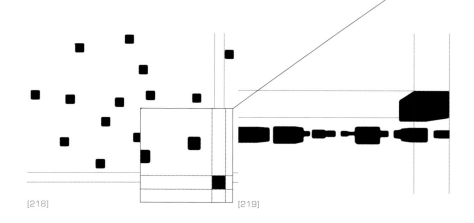

[218]　　　　　　　　　　　　[219]

A two-dimensional arrangement determines the grid for a three-dimensional scene. The 2D structure of the square has been transformed into the third dimension, like a floor plan.

A 2D grid can also determine the order in a three-dimensional space. This example shows how a grid determines the position of a figure on a flat surface. In addition to the order on the surface of a navigation unit for interactive television broadcasts, the grid also controls the order in space.

The grid is transformed in space, and determines the position of so-called »knowledge cubes« that the user can access directly by means of the navigation matrix.

At first a moderator in the centre of the »virtual studio« is responsible for the steering or the selection of the cube and thus the topic – each cube contains one topic. The chosen cube can be grabbed and will then disclose its contents.

This example shows the vertical, the horizontal and the diagonal room axes as ordering principles for multimedia content.

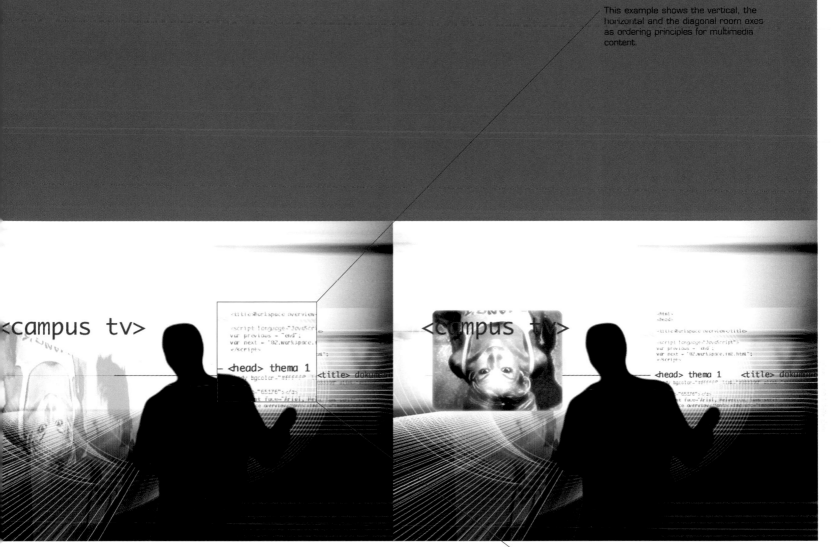

[220/1]

[220/2]

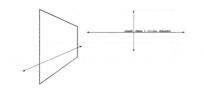

[221/1]

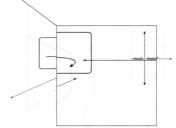

[221/2]

3D grids can also be created by structuring spatial units, just like 2D grids are used to structure flat surface units. The individual space segments are assigned specific functional units such as text, image, or moving pictures. In the animation the desired data will be produced at the appropriate place. This sort of grid is often used for interactive applications or for the creation of virtual studio environments.

This example shows how the space constants – vertical, horizontal, and diagonal – are used as ordering criteria for media contents. It is a virtual studio environment which offers the moderator the opportunity to select individual contents by touch. All the clip sequences are placed on a diagonal. They move from the space towards the moderator and are faded in on contact. The area for the selection of topics is horizontally aligned, the projection of text is positioned vertically.

[217/1–2] Virtual studio, space as an interface
[218] 2D grid set in space
[219] 2D grid transformed into the 3rd dimension, like a floor plan
[220/1–2] Virtual studio, space as an interface
[221/1–2] 3D grid, functional segmentation of space

basic grids

>2D GRIDS 3D GRIDS >4D GRIDS

Complex 3D grids focus on the effects that changes in space or objects have on other objects

GRID: Complex 3D grid
PRINCIPLE: Using complex 3D grids to influence space and objects
METHOD: Deforming space
EXAMPLE: Motion graphics
CONTEXT: 024, 076, 092, 106, 158
MOVIES: 222.mov, 223.mov

[222.mov/1]

complex 3d grid

Complex 3D grids can only be created using digital tools. A complex 3D grid is produced by generating
the effects of one object on another. This then regulates the behaviour and appearance of objects in
space on the basis of parameter transfer. Visible or invisible components of a spatial animation can
interact. The property or the behaviour of an object in a three-dimensional space has an effect on several
or all other objects in the same space. The object giving the impulse for the 3D grid can be visible or
invisible. It is also possible to place parameters in »empty« space.

If the space in which something is animated is distorted, then this distortion also affects the animated
object. A complex 3D grid can be produced by combining one or more objects that act on each other to
determine the overall behaviour and the dramaturgy of the animation.

Using this method involving manipulation of space and objects, it is possible to generate exciting rule-
based operations for the grid and thus for the animation. The fact that object parameters can be
transferred to other objects using the grid can lead to the generation of interesting chain reactions.

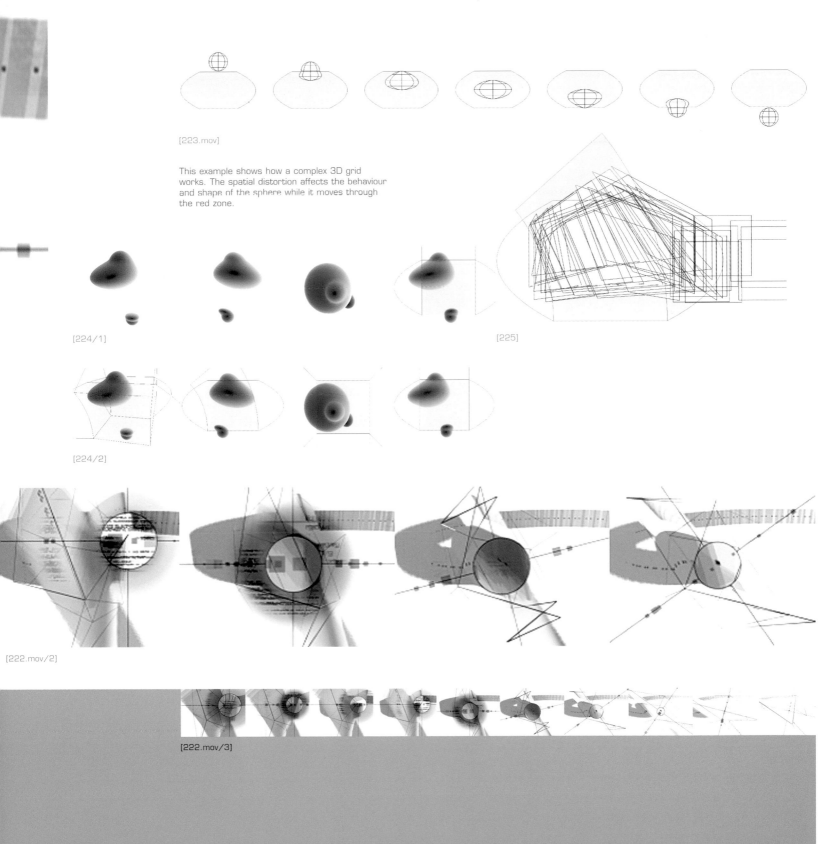

[223.mov]

This example shows how a complex 3D grid works. The spatial distortion affects the behaviour and shape of the sphere while it moves through the red zone.

[224/1]

[225]

[224/2]

[222.mov/2]

[222.mov/3]

[222.mov/1] Still from an animation created with a 3D grid
[223.mov] Sphere deformed by a complex 3D grid
[224/1] Deformed object from 4 sides
[224/2] Deformed object from 4 sides with visible 3D grid
[225] Square deformed by a complex 3D grid (timeslicing view)
[222.mov/2-3] Sequences from an animation created with a 3D grid

basic grids

>2D GRIDS 3D GRIDS >4D GRIDS

Complex 3D grids can affect individual objects or the space as a whole

GRID: Complex 3D grid
PRINCIPLE: Using complex 3D grids to influence space and objects
METHOD: Deforming space
EXAMPLE: Typographic animation
CONTEXT: 024, 076, 092, 106, 158
MOVIE: 226.mov

This example shows how the original vertical level is changed by a deformation. The grid (the deformation) affects the sphere. When parts of the sphere are outside the distorted level they return to the original shape. This grid does not affect the whole space.

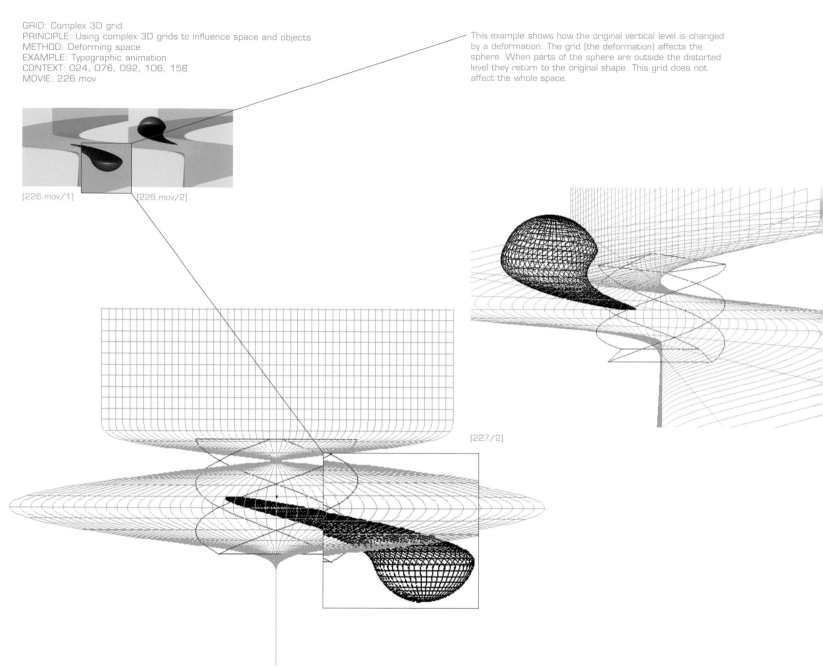

[226.mov/1]   [226.mov/2]

[227/2]

[227/1]

It is easy to see the effect of a grid and its contruction when watching a geometrical object. But if the method of 3D grids is applied to more complex arrangements of graphic elements, like typography, then this rapidly leads to animations that show no trace of the original grid. In this way sets of stylest can be drawn up that almost appear to make the manual setting of key frames superfluous.

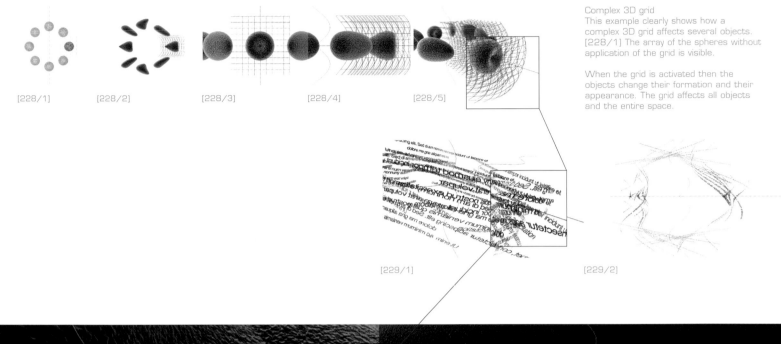

[228/1]   [228/2]   [228/3]   [228/4]   [228/5]

Complex 3D grid
This example clearly shows how a complex 3D grid affects several objects. [228/1] The array of the spheres without application of the grid is visible.

When the grid is activated then the objects change their formation and their appearance. The grid affects all objects and the entire space.

[229/1]   [229/2]

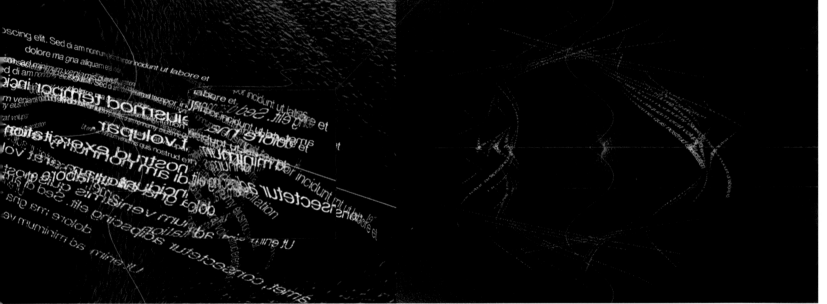

[230/1]   [230/2]

[231/2]

[232]

basic grids

Simple 4D grids are often based on self-defined rules which aim to create tension by a characteristic timing

GRID: 4D grid
PRINCIPLE: Modification of visual rythm
METHOD: Creating expectation by changing intervals
EXAMPLE: Typographic animation/motion graphics
CONTEXT: 018, 022, 024, 050, 066, 106, 124
MOVIE: 233.mov

TIP [The method of counting in can be used to build up the viewer's expectations.]

[234/1] ~

[233.mov/1], [234/2]

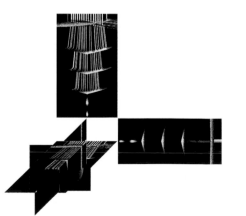

[233.mov/2]

simple 4d grids

4D grids, similar to the 3D grids can also be subdivided into two different types. The key feature of a 4D grid is that the animation is always determined primarily by the time factor. »Laws« or »rules« are set up for the time schedules within the animation.

For example, a simple 4D grid is used when graphic elements have to be shown or not shown with a specific rhythm. The dramaturgy is determined by the time; and this determines the nature of the animation. If the set of rules is dependent on points of time, then there is a simple 4D grid. Usually animations in space or on a plane surface are given a very basic 4D grid, in the sense that a 2D or 3D grid includes requirements about handling time. Mostly there will be a combination of 2D and 4D grid, or 3D and 4D grid. An animation with unvarying movements and speeds would soon seem very boring for the viewers.

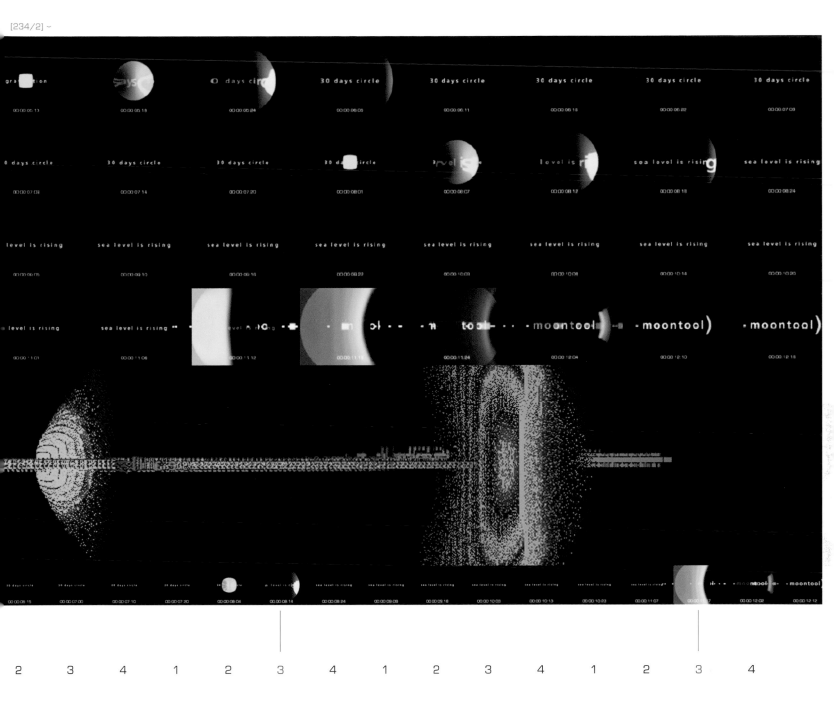

rhythm and typography

Animations that work with text must always ensure that the text is legible. The exposure time must be long enough. At the same time, the dramaturgy must offer more than just »one text after another«. Animations that have no accents can be boring, and the viewer's attention starts to wander.

In order to create a dramaturgy and also to ensure that the typography can be read, this animation has 3 different accents within a total of 6 beats. The animation is based on the idea of counting in, allowing the visual presentation of each beat. The viewer sees the first two circles appear, and is in a state of anticipation which is rewarded with the third beat.

The circle grows larger and typography is faded out exactly on the beat when the circles appear. This has the effect in this version that the timing for the opaque yellow circle is already different from that for the first two. In this case the beat is kept by the circle containing the typography.

When typography appears, the timing between the accents changes. Slowing down the timing gives the viewer the opportunity to read the text, but still to feel that the animation is following the original rhythm.

The length of the time change between beat 4 and beat 6 depends on the length of the text. If the text is longer, then the viewer will need more time to read it.

[233.mov/1] Visual analysis of the sequence's timing
[233.mov/2] Analysis of the animation, z axis exchanged with the time-axis
[234/1] Sequence of an animation which uses a 4D grid (counting in)
[234/2] Sequence overview of the animation

Replacing the z axis by the time axis leads to a
display which visualises a time sequence within
one image. The motifs at the sides of the cube are
created by placing the individual frame edges of
the animation next to each other. It is a pixel-by-
pixel addition of all frames which generates this
image, or a still from a video analysis.

[235] Volumetric illustration of a sequential process

basic grids

>2D GRIDS >3D GRIDS 4D GRIDS

Complex 4D grids are often based on the manipulation of the element's dynamics or of temporary periods of time

GRID: Complex 4D grid
PRINCIPLE: Using complex 4D grids to transform the order of time frames
METHOD: Manipulating temporary periods of time
EXAMPLE: Manipulation of real footage
CONTEXT: 018, 022, 024, 046, 088, 124, 164
MOVIE: 241.mov

This example shows a 4D grid created by the technique of displacement. That means that the temporal changes of the motif's speed were automatically generated by using the luminance value of this »displacement map«. It is the impulse and the control for the change of time within the motif. Where the illustration is darker, the red lines move more slowly [238, 239]. This creates a position-based (depending on the place of the dark area) speed manipulation for each frame.

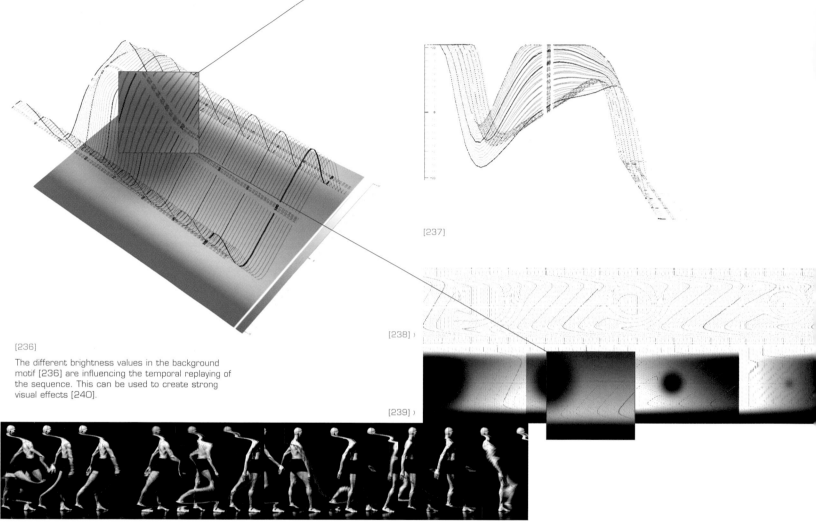

[237]

[236]

The different brightness values in the background motif [236] are influencing the temporal replaying of the sequence. This can be used to create strong visual effects [240].

[238] ›

[239] ›

[240]

complex 4d grid

The complex 4D grid is a powerful grid. It determines the temporal manipulation of the speed, the appearance over time or the rhythm of graphical elements or any other individual levels or elements. Basically, this means that individual time segments of the animation are manipulated. This can be automated or done manually. This method is often used in typographic animations and animations with a complex interplay of graphical elements. It can define changes of pace very precisely. These lead to a faster or slower speed of the objects or the replaying of the animations as a whole (cf. dramaturgy). Depending on the programs used, complex 4D grids can be created in a variety of ways.

Complex 4D grids are often developed by analysing the visual properties of artwork, samples or behaviours. The displacing method can be used as an automatic way to create the data to define or control a temporary manipulation of footage changes.

[241.mov/1]

The original material, the footage of a head turning to the right, was partly changed by means of the 4D grid. Within a defined zone (red), a pixel-wide line from the previous frame was inserted into each frame.

[242]

Over time, the target moves from bottom to top through the grid, so all pixel lines added are placed between the original image and the final image.

[243/1–2]

The temporal sequence becomes visible at the sides of the cube. The z axis has been replaced by the time axis.

RULE [25 fps x 1 pixel = 25 pixels per second, i.e. the animation lasts 4 seconds if a distance of 100 pixels is covered.]

One vertical pixel line was taken from every frame of the original image sequence and inserted into the current frame. Placing these pixel lines alongside each other in the present frame creates a view of the past or the future if the pixel lines are taken from the following frames.

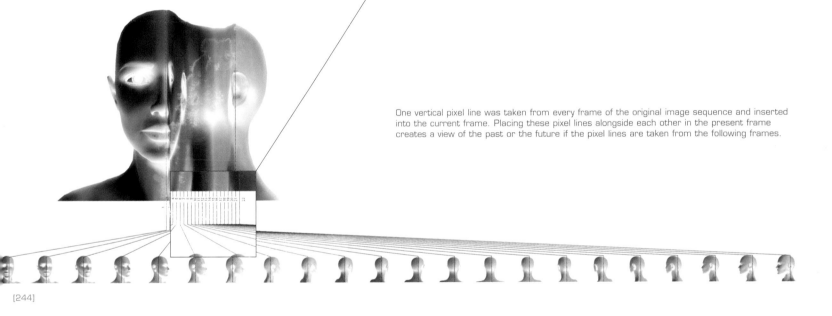

[244]

This principle of designing is based on the manipulation of time sequences. One part of the frame from the past was added into the current frame. Therefore exactly one pixel line was defined, so that only this was pasted into the current frame. This method was used continuously. Each pixel line was moved one pixel to the left, so that the pixel lines add up. This adding of the line in each frame affects simultaneously the temporary length of the animation. As per frame respectively one vertical pixel line was added and the zone in which this happens is 100 pixels wide, the duration of the animation can be counted (see above).

[236] Visualisation of a complex 4D grid
[237] Influencing relative time by the luminance of the model
[238] Time grid, time deformation is visible
[239] Luminance of the background motif influences time
[240] Sequence with visible time grid
[241.mov/1] Still from an animation with a 4D grid
[242] Illustration of the principle of a complex 4D grid
[243/1–2] Volumetric illustration of a sequential process
[244] Illustration of the principle of a complex 4D grid

basic grids

>2D GRIDS >3D GRIDS 4D GRIDS

Complex 4D grids can be gained from an analysis of most disparate data

GRID: Complex 4D grid
PRINCIPLE: Creation of a 4D grid by tracking
METHOD: Manipulating temporary periods of time by analysing audio
EXAMPLE: Synchronising speech and typography
CONTEXT: 016, 018, 022, 024, 046, 088, 124
MOVIE: 245.mov

RULE [As words are spoken faster than they can be read, the 4D grid was multiplied by a factor of 5 before use. This means that the text can be comfortably read.]

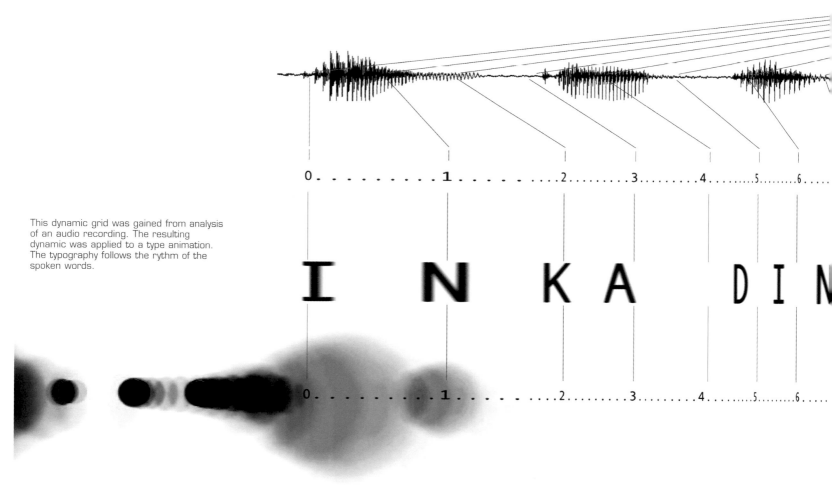

This dynamic grid was gained from analysis of an audio recording. The resulting dynamic was applied to a type animation. The typography follows the rythm of the spoken words.

complex 4D grid

Many 4D grids are used in the form of tracking data. The 4D grid is extracted from the analysis of various objects/movements and used as the basis for a 4D grid for other elements. 4D grids are used to control graphic elements and very easily generate dynamics that have significant effects.

This time grid was extracted from the audio recording of the spoken word and is used as a »template« in order to determine the dynamics of graphics or typography. The dynamic time grid describes temporary changes of speed within an animation. Depending on the dramaturgy, the graphic elements will be animated more quickly or more slowly.

The time grid from the audio recordings can be applied to the typography to determine the dynamic of the text. In other words, the set-up speed of the text is distorted by the relative time of the original reading flow. Applying the time grid to graphic elements results in a very dynamic and harmonious animation. In this case the inner logic of the grid is not visible.

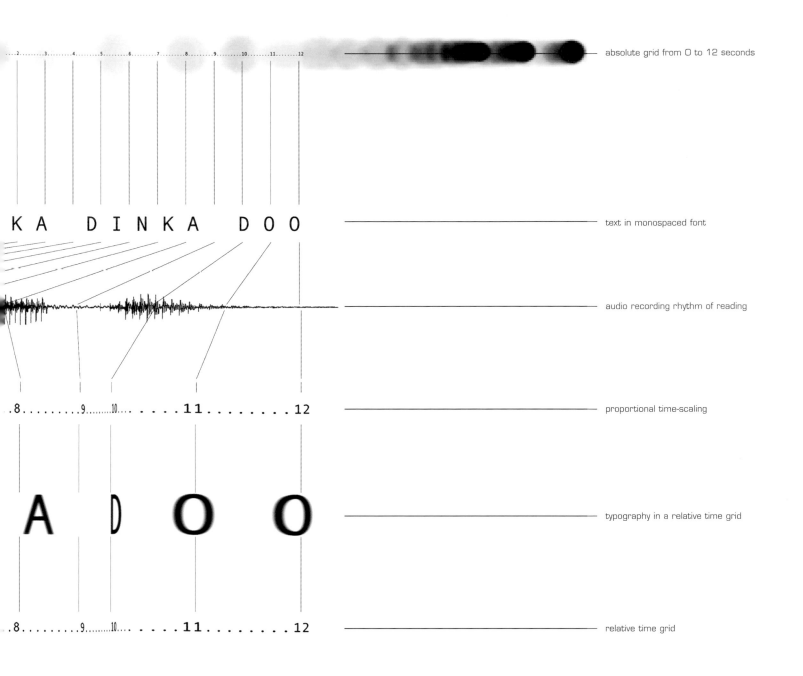

absolute grid from 0 to 12 seconds

text in monospaced font

audio recording rhythm of reading

proportional time-scaling

typography in a relative time grid

relative time grid

[245.mov]

[245.mov] Schematic illustration of the compilation of a time grid, e.g. by audio analysis

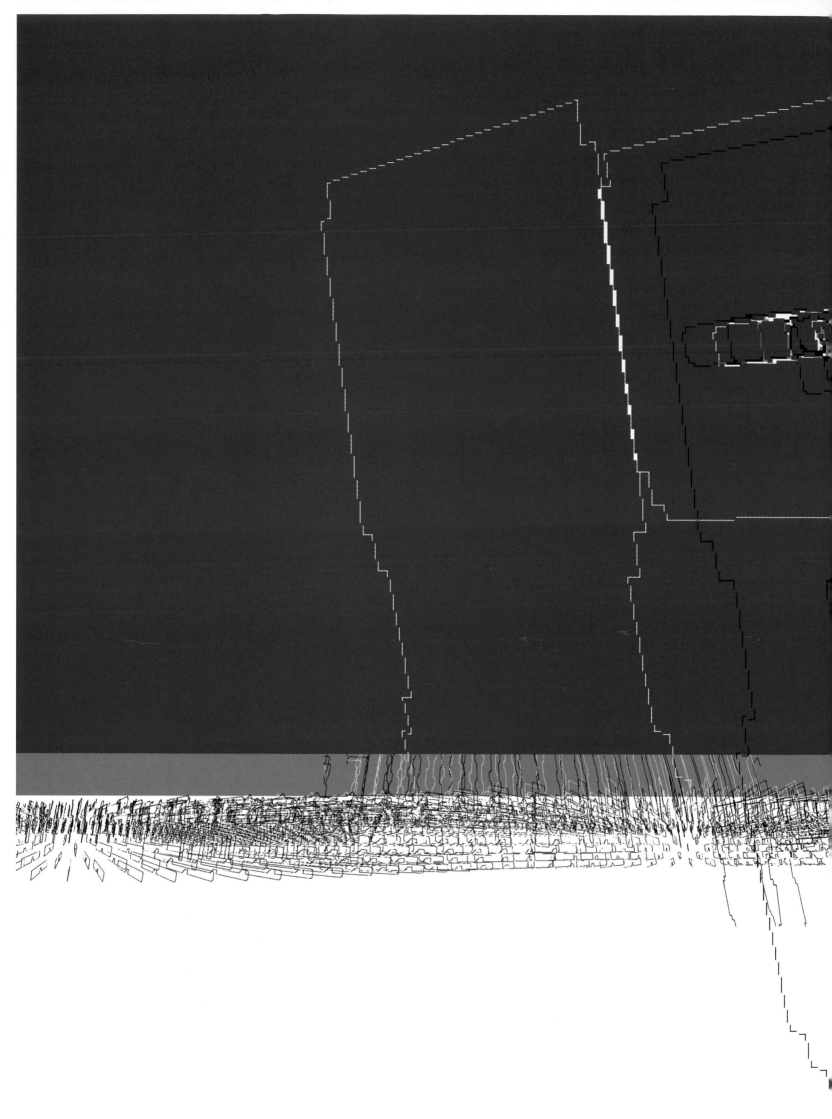

tracking

tracking

A very interesting and effective way to generate grid systems for animations is the principle of tracking. Grid systems based on tracking are generally derived from reality. The idea is to analyse real objects, processes, movements, or modes of behaviour, and to use the values obtained as a grid to control graphic elements or layers. Various parameters of one object, that determine its behaviour (movement, speed, etc.) are transferred to another element. Reality is taken as a model or pattern. When it changes, then there is also a change in the animation.

One form of tracking that is easy to understand is motion tracking. A movement, like for example a person walking, is captured with motion capturing. The changes in position of the body and extremities are recorded with tracked points. Later, in the grid, they serve as »anchor points« for graphical elements which will stick exactly to the tracked points and behave the same.

The tracking method is a quick way to create interesting time/space »templates« for the behaviour of graphical elements or layers in animations. In addition to the positioning in time and space, information is also obtained about the timing of the elements, which can also be transferred to the graphical elements. The following chapter provides an insight into some methods of tracking.

tracking

PROPERTY >MOVEMENT >STRUCTURE >BEHAVIOUR >INTERACTION >AUDIO

Property tracking refers to the process of analysing and transferring values of various object
properties such as changes in size, colour and shape to other elements

GRID: Complex 4D grid
PRINCIPLE: Using value changes of an element's properties as a grid
METHOD: Tracking of properties
EXAMPLE: Motion graphic footage
CONTEXT: 016, 046, 086, 088
MOVIE: –

[301/1]

[301/2]

property tracking

In this book we will be distinguishing between various ways of generating grids. Property tracking is the method of transferring values for the properties of individual graphical objects to chosen parameters of other objects. Property tracking is one of the few tracking methods that not only makes use of real footage but can also be based solely on sources of digital data. Properties of the objects are directly or indirectly linked to properties of other objects.

The links can range from very simple to highly complex ones. This depends on what »rules« govern the links, or the parameters that are associated with the value.

For example, a change in brightness of one object can affect the size of another object. That would be a very simple grid (see also chapter 5). Things get slightly more complicated if the effect is not directly proportional. The complexity of a grid is determined by the »set of rules« governing the links. An interesting example is when object properties are transferred to modes of behaviour.

The process that is referred here to as »property tracking«, in which the values of the properties of graphics or film elements are analysed and transferred to the values of other properties, is the basis for a frequently used process known as displacing.

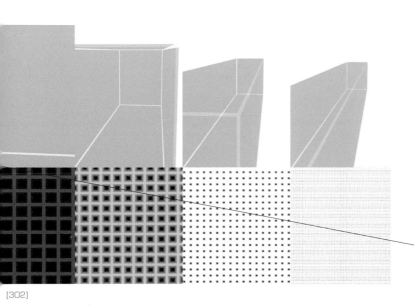

RULE [The darker the red field becomes, the more particles are generated.]

[302]

[301/1] The brightness controls the number of particles.
[301/2] The brightness controls the number of particles.
[302] Sample size or brightness controls the viewing distance.

tracking

>PROPERTY MOVEMENT >STRUCTURE >BEHAVIOUR >INTERACTION >AUDIO

An absolutely fundamental technique for the creation of grids for moving pictures is to develop grids on the basis of motion analysis
Motion tracking refers to the parametric transfer of x, y, z coordinates and timing

GRID: Complex 4D grid
PRINCIPLE: Using movement paths as a grid for time and space
METHOD: Capturing of motion, tracking of motion
EXAMPLE: Character animation: karate fighter, emulating walking
CONTEXT: 018, 028, 038, 046, 124, 140
MOVIE: 304.mov

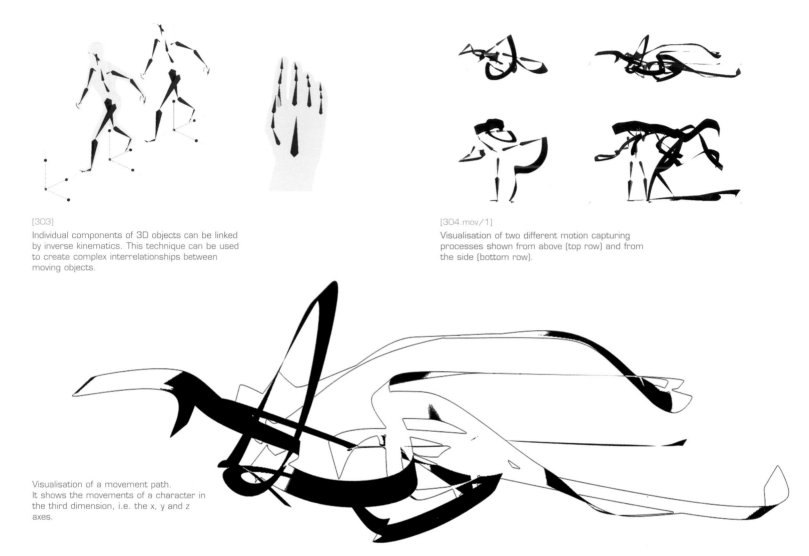

[303]
Individual components of 3D objects can be linked
by inverse kinematics. This technique can be used
to create complex interrelationships between
moving objects.

[304.mov/1]
Visualisation of two different motion capturing
processes shown from above (top row) and from
the side (bottom row).

Visualisation of a movement path.
It shows the movements of a character in
the third dimension, i.e. the x, y and z
axes.

[305]

motion capturing

It would be extremely complicated to create a digital simulation of living beings
by hand because of the complexity and dynamism of real movement processes.
The process of motion capturing is a method which is used to derive dynamic
grids quickly and efficiently from the analysis of real movement processes.

The aim is to record movement processes of real living beings and then to
transfer them to virtual characters. On the one hand this saves time in the
creation of the animation, and on the other hand it also provides a maximum of
authenticity of movement.

To this end, the person or other living being has markers attached to the joints
or limbs. Then the movements of the person or living being are filmed.

With the appropriate programs and processing methods, the space-time
»track« of the movement of individual limbs can be extracted (by recording the
x, y and z coordinates and the time). This information is used in the area of
character animation to control the movement of the »virtual character«. The
aim is usually to achieve a 1:1 transfer of the results from the real living being
to the virtual character.

Transferring parameters from one object to another is the basic principle of all
tracking methods. Parameters gained from analysis are always transferred to
other objects and used to control their movements and timing. This clearly
shows how dynamic and three-dimensional grids are generated and used in the
area of moving picture design. Numerous grid principles can be described on
the basis of this principle.

This illustration shows a figure whose motion paths have been made visible. The
motion pattern of this figure was gained by capturing the motion of a real
karate fighter which was subsequently assigned to the figure as a »motion
template«. In this way, the type as well as dynamics of the motion is determined
by the analysed space-time-coordinates of the real-life karate fighter.

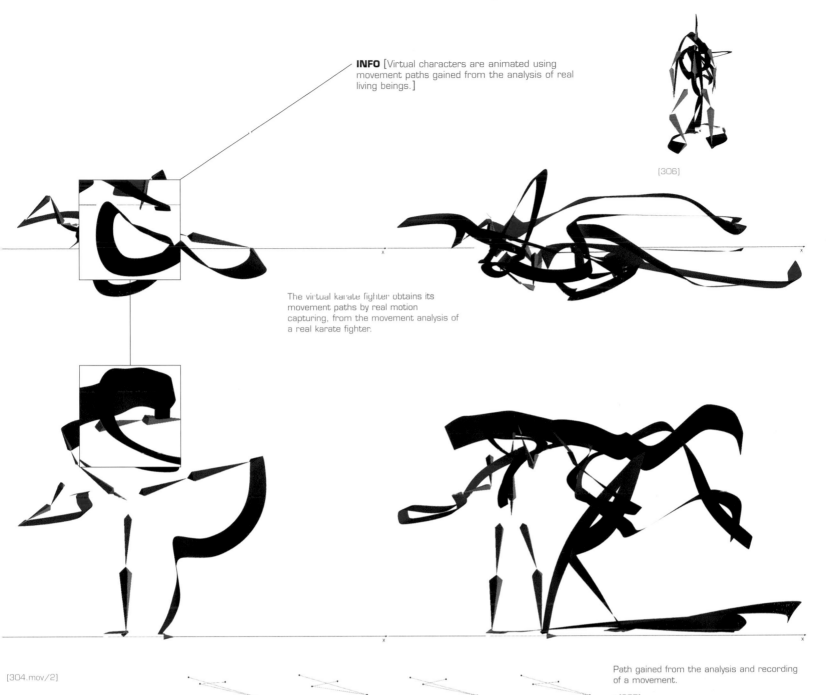

INFO [Virtual characters are animated using movement paths gained from the analysis of real living beings.]

[306]

The virtual karate fighter obtains its movement paths by real motion capturing, from the movement analysis of a real karate fighter.

[304.mov/2]

Path gained from the analysis and recording of a movement.

‹ [307]

[308] ›

motion tracking

In contrast to motion capturing, motion tracking is used to link graphic and cinematographic elements to the moving objects and motifs within films and animations. A number of points on an object in the footage are marked and the movement of these points is analysed. This gives a pathway or a sequence of key frames that can be used as a matrix for the control of the dynamics and dramaturgy of other elements. Motion tracking involves extracting the sequence of movements of the objects from the footage and then applying these to other elements.

This method can be used very well as a dynamic grid. In particular when the original material (footage) will not form a visible part of the subsequent animation.

As a rule, real footage is the original material used, because genuine sequences of movements contain patterns with which we are all very familiar. If these are then transferred to abstract graphics or typography then this results in animations that have a dramaturgy that seems familiar to the viewer.

This example [308] has a number of interesting aspects. The figures in the animation originate from a program that was developed to generate human animations. The motion data and patterns were gathered from the analysis of real human movements. The classic motion capturing was employed. In this way, pure digital motion sequences were generated that were very realistic. In the next step, the digital character animation was used as the motion tracking object. The movement was analysed again and transferred to graphic elements, points and lines. Since the tracking footage can still be seen in the example, the principle is easy to follow.

[303] Creating interrelationships by inverse kinematics
[304.mov/1] Views of two motion capturing processes
[305] Illustration of a motion capturing path
[306] View of motion capturing and fighter at the end of the session
[304.mov/2] Views of two motion capturing processes
[307] Movement paths in motion tracking
[308] Extract from a motion tracking sequence

tracking

Four-point tracking is a very well-known form of motion tracking. It is often used in post-production

GRID: Complex 4D grid
PRINCIPLE: Using multiple movement points/paths as grid
METHOD: Tracking of four points in motion
EXAMPLE: Four-point tracking
CONTEXT: 028, 038, 046, 154
MOVIE: 308.mov

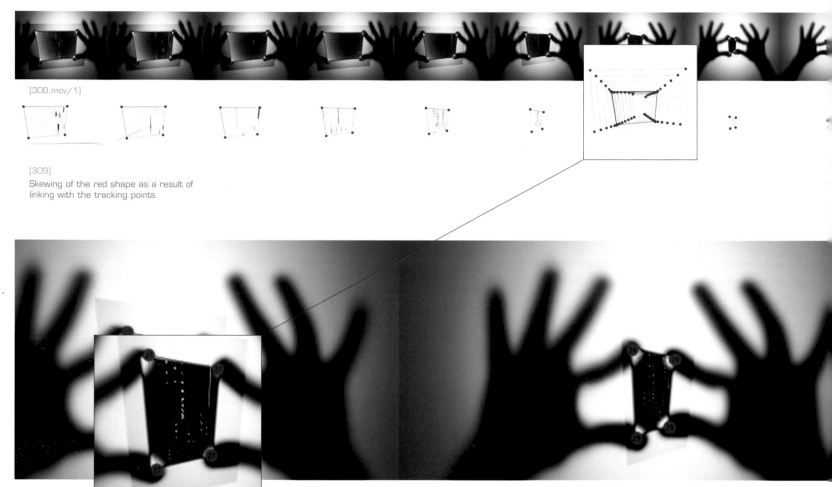

[308.mov/1]

[309]
Skewing of the red shape as a result of
linking with the tracking points.

[308.mov/2]

four-point tracking

Four-point tracking is a special form of motion tracking and is used for example to insert additional sequences in real footage. Since usually the objects that are to serve as the carrier medium or as the projection area are themselves dynamic, the technique of four-point tracking is used to register the dynamics of the object frame by frame. As the name suggests, four suitable points are marked on the target object. In reality this can be done by sticking points on the person or object in question, or it can be done in post-production by digital tracking.

This procedure makes it possible to link the object and the projection image. In this way, the material to be projected can be placed exactly within the four points. In addition it also takes on the dynamics since it is »attached« to the markings, rather like the 2D paths.

This example shows four-point tracking of two fingers. This is used to later generate a virtual area between the hands. The straight presentation of the tracking results show the movements of the finger markings over time. A graphic was assigned to these points, which then follows precisely the changes of the reference points. The movements of the hands thus provides the grid for the graphics.

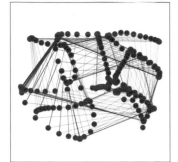

If four-point tracking is carried out not only on the flat surface but also in a spatial context, this can lead to very dynamic and complex movement paths.

[310]

INFO [Four-point tracking originally comes from classical post-production. It offers a good basis to develop creative concepts, by using it as a grid.]

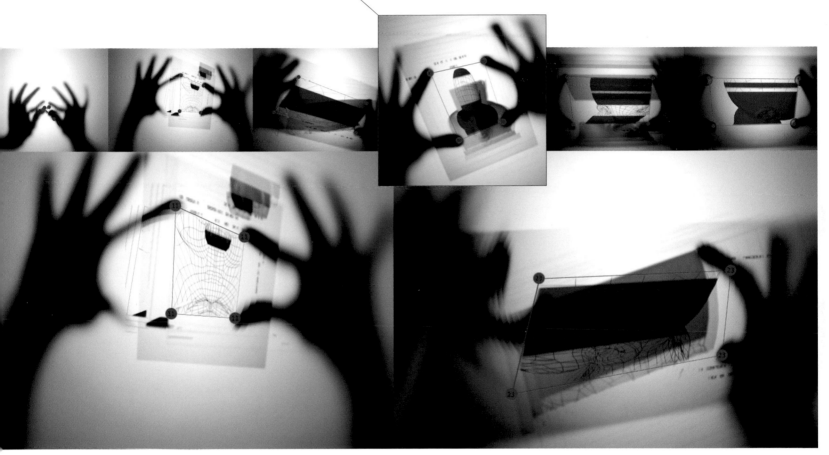

[311]

Attaching sequences to other sequences seems fairly straightforward. A simple zoom or lifting of areas is not difficult to comprehend. But things are different if complex movements are to take place during the tracking. For example, if the projection area itself is dynamic, then the tracking changes considerably. The information about the angle of rotation and the inclination then becomes relevant. Depending on the data, the projection area will not only change in size but also in shape and inclination. The time sequence shown in one picture clearly demonstrates the spatial dynamics of the grid.

[308.mov/1] Sequence of four-point tracking
[309] Grid sequence of four-point tracking
[308.mov/2] Stills from four-point tracking
[310] Movement sequence of dynamic four-point tracking
[311] Sequence and style of four-point tracking in the spatial dimension

tracking

>PROPERTY **MOVEMENT** >STRUCTURE >BEHAVIOUR >INTERACTION >AUDIO

Motion tracking might be implemented in a minimal form as one-point tracking

GRID: Complex 4D grid
PRINCIPLE: Using movement and rotating as grid
METHOD: Tracking of one point
EXAMPLE: One-point tracking
CONTEXT: 028, 038, 046, 133
MOVIE: 312.mov

TIP [One-point tracking offers numerous possibilities for use in spite of the minimal tracking. In addition to transferring the x and y coordinates, the values for the angle, rotation and size of the tracking point can also be transformed.]

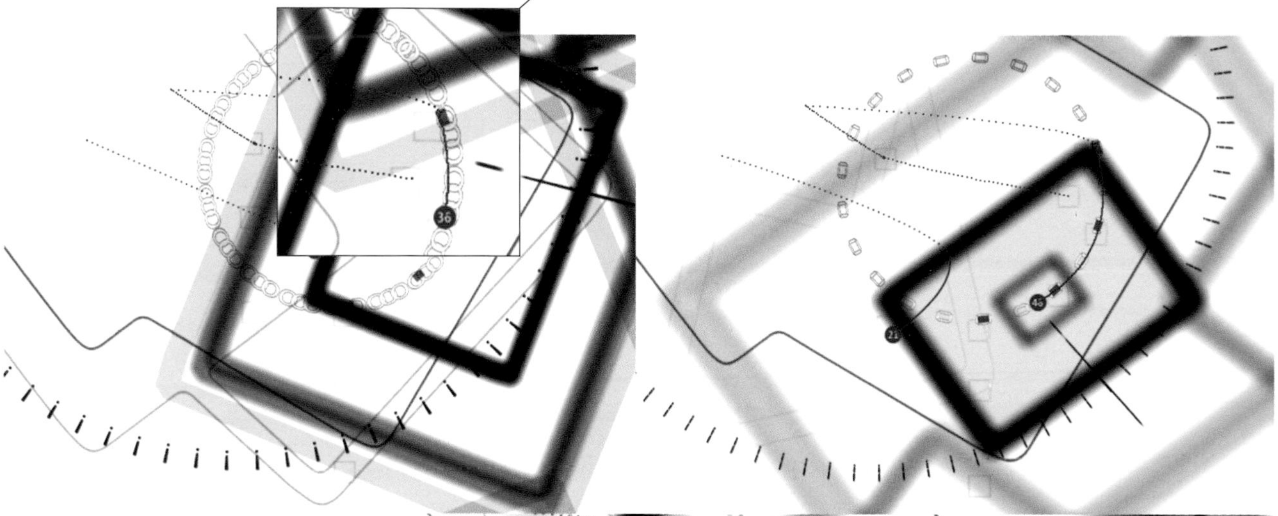

Visualisation of the grid generated by the various angles of the touch point.

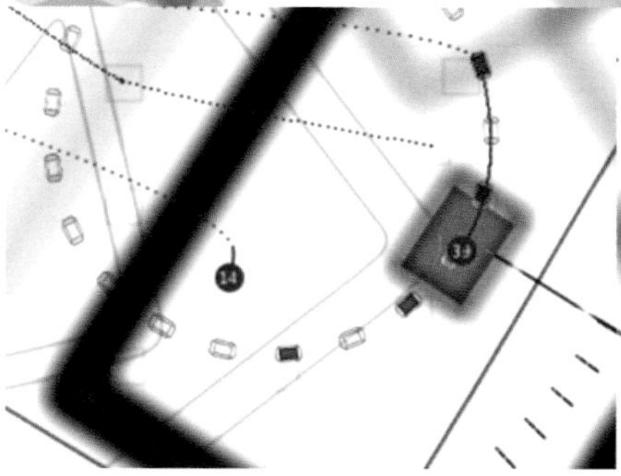

‹ [312.mov/1–2]

[312.mov/3]

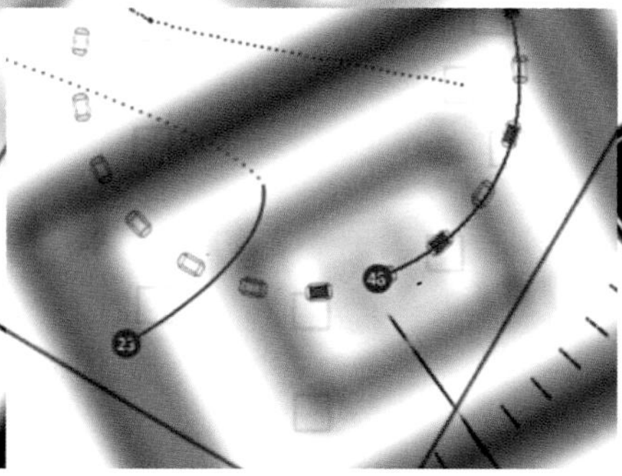

[312.mov/4]

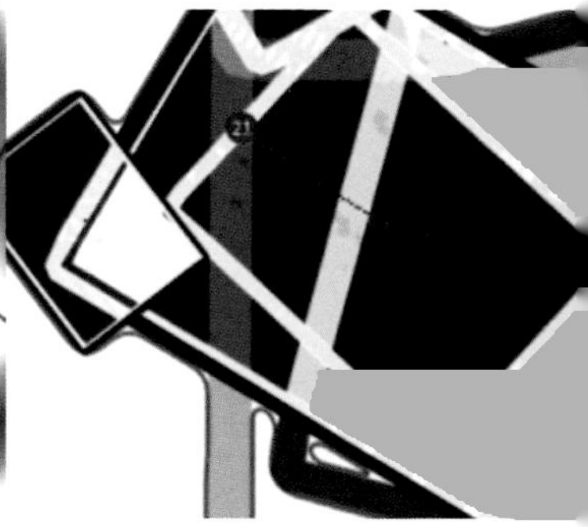

[312.mov/5]

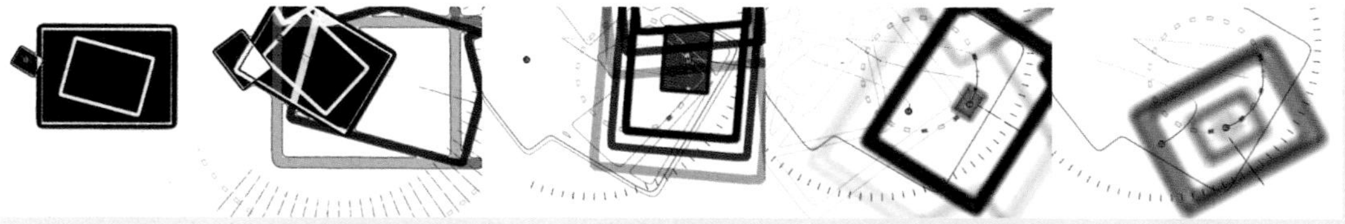

[312.mov/6]

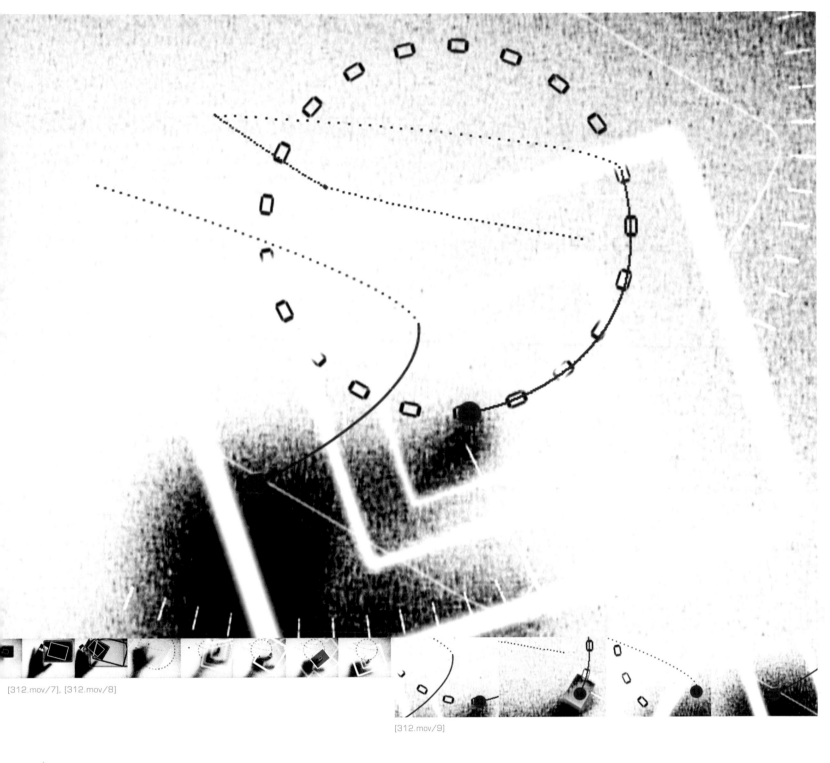

[312.mov/7], [312.mov/8]

[312.mov/9]

one-point tracking

Tracking objects can be carried out with as many points as required. For example, if only one point is used to track then in addition to the movement over a surface or in space, the angle of rotation can also be used to control graphic elements. In this example, the resolution or lack of resolution of the tracking point on the finger is used to generate graphic objects. If the finger touches the glass plate, then new frameworks are formed at that point that then follow the path of the tracking point. The angle of rotation determines the rotation of the frames.

[312.mov/1–6] Stills from the grid sequence in one-point tracking
[312.mov/7–9] Stills and sequence of one-point tracking

tracking

>PROPERTY >MOVEMENT STRUCTURE >BEHAVIOUR >INTERACTION >AUDIO

Structure tracking refers to the parametric transfer of values gained from structure or process analysis

GRID: Complex 4D grid
PRINCIPLE: Using structure changes as grid
METHOD: Tracking of a structure
EXAMPLE: Animation of datagraphics
CONTEXT: 016, 018, 046, 086
MOVIE: –

[313/1]

structure tracking

The method of generating a grid by tracking structures (processes) is based on the assumption that the essentials, the characteristic features of the behaviour of objects, people, animals, processes, etc., lie in their structure, and the aim is to extract these and transfer them to other media, in the form of a grid to control graphic elements. It is usually necessary to work with a combination of various factors. For example, in addition to movement and dynamics it is also possible to analyse sound, or completely abstract changes as the basis for a grid. Grid impulses of an animation could be stock market fluctuations, weather reports, or traffic levels. Structure tracking, like all other tracking methods can be used to analyse numerical values from processes and to transfer these to other processes in order to induce changes.

The values obtained from the analysis control graphic elements. It is then no longer necessary to set key frames directly. As in other cases it is possible to produce grids at various levels of complexity – different elements can be transferred at the same time with different systems of rules. The process is easy to follow if a numerical value is transferred directly, so that a share value is linked to the size of text.

An indirect transfer of a share value to the dynamic movement of a graphic element requires an additional transfer rule, for example the higher the value the slower the movement, or the higher the value the closer the element moves to the edge of the screen. Alternatively, the element might begin to move more quickly vertically. The hard part when developing effective grids from tracking data is to choose the right »transfer rules«, that form a fundamental part of the final grid.

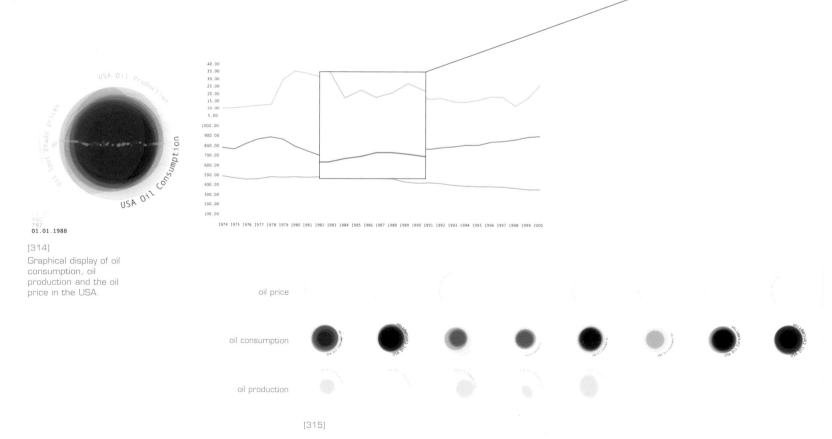

[314]
Graphical display of oil consumption, oil production and the oil price in the USA.

oil price

oil consumption

oil production

[315]

RULE [The greater the values of the data image, the larger the number and size of the circles or particles generated for each value.]

[313/2], [313/3–4]

Data about American oil consumption from 1974 to 2000 provides the basis for the structure tracking here. Information about the oil consumption, oil production, and the oil price numerically control the appearance and behaviour of graphic elements. Since the values have changed over the years, these changes could be used in order to steer an animation. At first the consumption, production and the price are assigned a graphic representation, in this case a turquoise circle, an olive-coloured circle, and a number of small, green »drops«. Their behaviour is controlled by the data from the analysis. At first the highest and lowest values are determined, and the relative changes within this band are used to steer the graphics. So their behaviour relates to the relative difference between the highest and the lowest value.

The number and size of the turquoise circles increases the greater the oil consumption is. Similarly, when production increases, the number of circles also increases. Since these are translucent, the overlapping parts form a dark area. The change in prices is visualised in the horizontal array. The drops rise and fall as the price changes.

[315/2]

[313/1] Stills from a structure tracking animation
[314] Model for a structure tracking
[315/1] Visual change of the individual layers
[313/2] Sequence from a structure tracking animation
[313/3–4] Stills from a structure tracking animation
[315/2] Graphical elements/layers which represent values from structure tracking

tracking

Behaviour tracking refers to the parametric transfer of values gained from behaviour analysis

GRID: Complex 4D grid
PRINCIPLE: Using human behaviour as grid
METHOD: Tracking of perception
EXAMPLE: Typographic animation based on eye movement
CONTEXT: 018, 028, 042, 046, 134
MOVIE: 316.mov

The red display [316.mov/1] shows an animation with inversely proportional parameter transfer of the x, y coordinates of the viewing movements to the x, y coordinates of the letters. As the coordinate in the animation containing the letters is fixed, an eye movement to the right is interpreted as a typographic animation to the left. The preceding sign of the tracking data is simply reversed. The tracking of the coordinates also records the behaviour of the viewer. This becomes visible in the timing of the animation.

[316.mov/1]

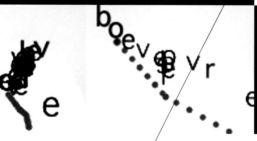

[317/1]   [317/2]   [317/3]

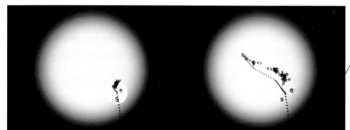

[318/1–7]

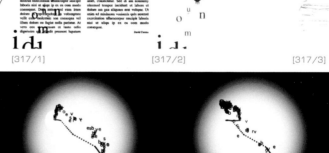

[318/8–10]

This example [318] shows an animation in which the grid was generated in a similar way to the red display, but has been used differently in the implementation. The duration and coordinates of the pixels viewed within a certain period provide the pulse for the generating of letters. The closer the area viewed is to the edge of the circle, the larger the letters appear.

RULE [Inversely proportional parameter transfer from the eye movement to the movement of the letter.]

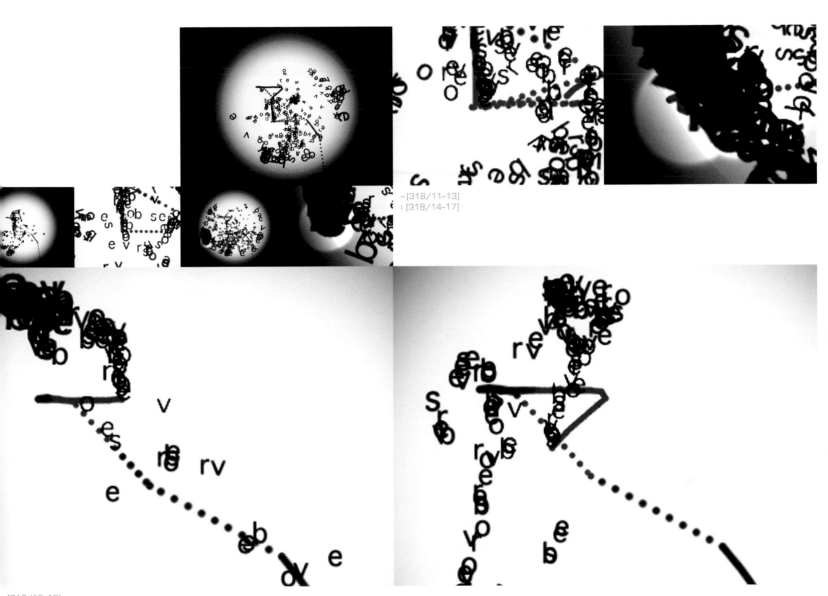

~[318/11–13]
([318/14–17]

[318/18–19]

behaviour tracking

Behaviour tracking can be seen as a mixed form combining motion tracking and structure tracking. Basically a motion or behaviour is tracked and used as a grid or as the basis for animations. However, the origin of the movement and the actions is relevant in this case, which is why the name behaviour tracking is used.

The idea is similar to that for structure tracking, namely that familiar patterns are extracted from behaviour, and these become even more apparent when they are transferred to other media and parameters. Behaviour tracking determines the x, y, and sometimes also the z coordinates, and at the same time the time grid.

The basis of this animation is a grid that is gained from the analysis of the viewing direction or reading direction of a person. The eye movements of a person reading a newspaper were recorded, and then used as a model for these typographic animations. Viewing angle analysis was used to obtain the x and y coordinates and the associated timing.

In these examples it seems relatively easy to recognise the underlying grid or principle. But if the text or the paths tracked become invisible, or if the parameters that have been gained are not transferred so directly, the operation of the grid will play a background role.

[316.mov/1] Stills showing behaviour tracking [eye tracking]
[317/1] Model of the eye tracking
[317/2–3] Display of the eye tracking path and typography of the animation
[318/1–19] Stills from behaviour tracking based on eye movement

tracking

Interaction tracking refers to the parametric transfer of values obtained in an analysis of interaction processes
(a mixture of behaviour tracking and structure tracking)

GRID: Complex 4D grid
PRINCIPLE: Using interaction as grid
METHOD: Tracking of the user's interaction
EXAMPLE: 3D search engine
CONTEXT: 018, 028, 042, 046
MOVIE: –

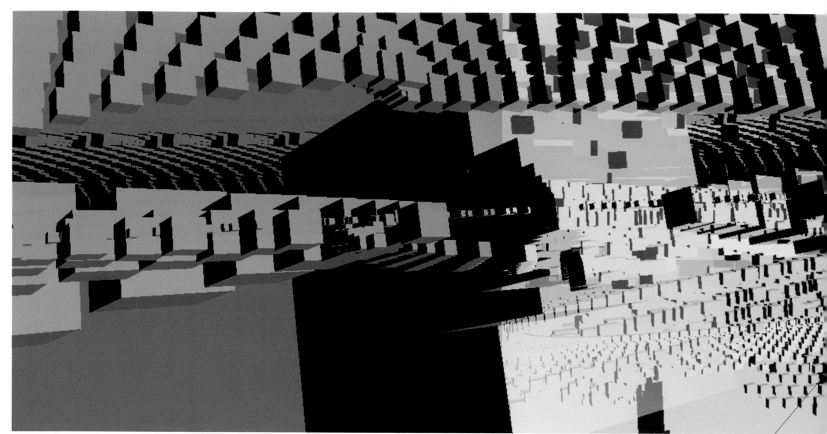

[319]

RULE [The movement, speed and position of
the 3D control generate more or less large
objects on its current x, y and z coordinates.]

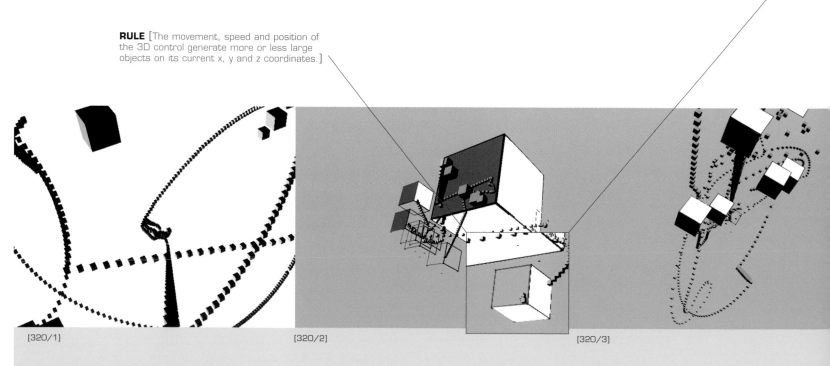

[320/1]   [320/2]   [320/3]

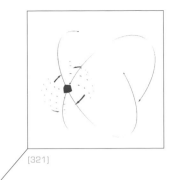

[321]

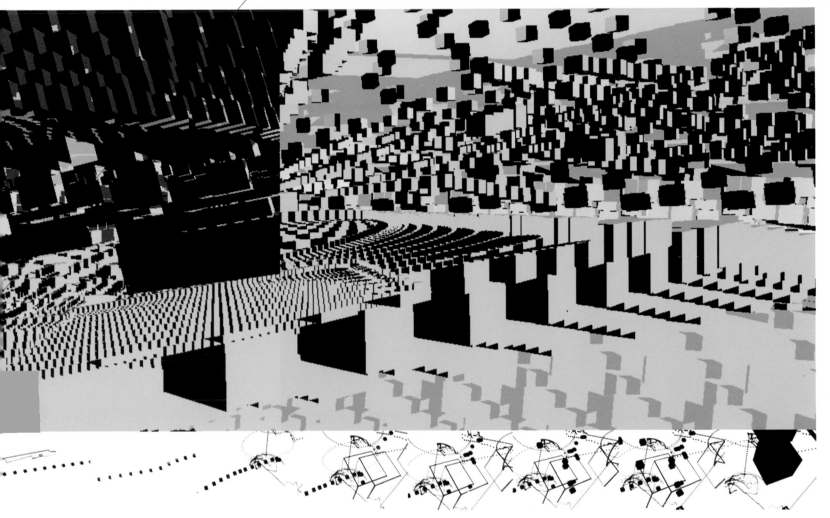

[322]

interaction trackinig

We define interaction tracking as a special form of behaviour tracking. With interaction tracking, any type of human behaviour can be used as a basis for a grid when using digital media. In this case, data is gathered from the analysis of the interaction processes to generate x, y, and possibly also z coordinates along a time-line, namely the duration of interaction. The data can be used directly or indirectly as a grid for graphic elements. But what sorts of interaction can be used?

One example might be the analysis of eye movements when looking at images, movies or websites. Another is direct interaction in the form of mouse movements and mouse clicks on a website, which could also be used to generate a grid. As with any other form of tracking, the data obtained can have a very direct effect, for example a direct transfer of the x, y, z coordinates to other graphic elements, or there can be more complex systems of rules, leading to indirect links and changes of properties such a colour or size.

[319] Still from interaction tracking
[320/1–3] Stills at the start of interaction tracking
[321] Movement in the third dimension
[322] Path generated by the user's movement as a sequence

tracking

Audio tracking refers to the parametric transfer of various values from audio data to image data

GRID: Complex 4D grid
PRINCIPLE: Using value changes of audio as grid
METHOD: Tracking of audio parameters
EXAMPLE: Audio-visual composition
CONTEXT: 016, 018, 042, 046
MOVIES: 323.mov, 328.mov

INFO [This audio-visual composition is based on an analysis of hyena calls. On the basis of the melody, a composition for 4 instruments was created. Each instrument is assigned a visual representation (layer). Parametric transfer of audio values (such as pitch, volume etc.) to image properties (such as brightness, size, etc.) creates an absolutely exact, automatically generated audio-visual animation.]

[323.mov/1]

[324]

[325] ›

[326] ›

[327] ›

[323.mov/1] Stills from audio-visual composition
[324] Extract from the audio wave form
[325] Horizontal cross-section through the centre of the animation
[326] Vertical cross-section through the centre of the animation
[327] Extract from the audio wave form
[328.mov] Volumetric display of various audio-visual compositions
[329] Stills from the audio-visual composition
[330] Extract from the audio wave form
[331] Horizontal cross-section through the centre of the animation
[332] Vertical cross-section through the centre of the animation
[333] Extract from the audio wave form

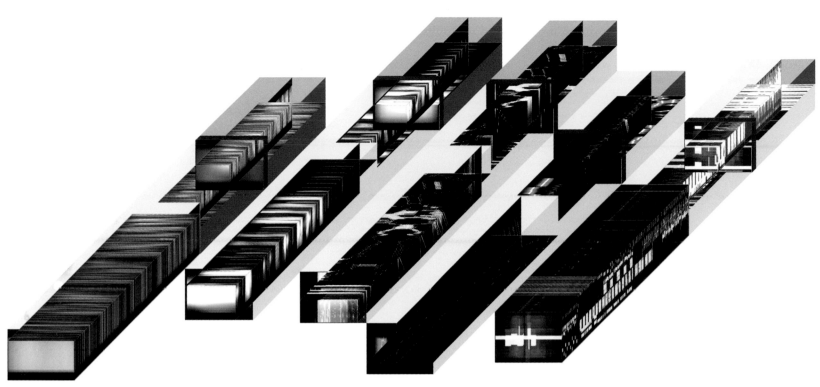

[328.mov]

[329], [330]

‹ [331]

‹ [332]

‹ [333]

audio tracking

Audio tracking is actually a special form of structure tracking, and like all the tracking methods described here it involves analysing parameter data and transferring them to parameters of graphical elements. Audio tracking is a means of extracting the properties of sound such as pitch, volume or dynamic playing techniques and using them to control images or their behaviour.

As in all forms of tracking, the data from the analysis can have a direct or indirect effect on the objects. The tracking can be transferred to the properties, the behaviour or the dynamics of the objects. As a rule, grids generated with audio tracking are combined with object tracking. This process means that the graphical elements used, like audio compositions, combine with each other and are interlinked.

tracking

Audio tracking refers to the transfer of parameters analysed from audio data

GRID: Complex 4D grid
PRINCIPLE: Using value changes of audio as grid
METHOD: Tracking of audio parameters
EXAMPLE: Audio-visual composition
CONTEXT: 016, 018, 042, 046
MOVIE: 334.mov

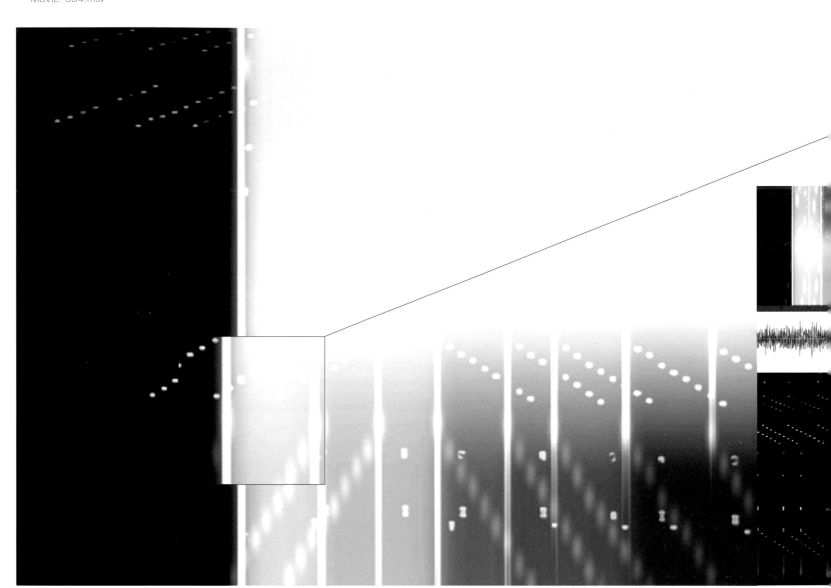

[334.mov/1]

This animation has a long history. It is based on the video recordings of a punched tape matrix for player pianos (automatic pianos). It shows a composition by Hans Haas No. 27.
Compositions for player pianos are taken down by metric recording as holes on a roll of paper. The paper runs over a pneumatic roller, and wherever there is a hole in the paper, a note is sounded. The high notes on the right, the low notes on the left. At the time when the composition is being played, only one line of the punched tape matrix is relevant – the line that is currently passing the tracker bar.

The principle of the player piano is actually based on the process of tracking. The pitch is determined by the horizontal position and the duration or frequency of the notes by the vertical position on the punched tape matrix, where these data are recorded by punching holes so that they can be played back. This process can be regarded as the predecessor of midi technology.

This animation is at face value only indirectly a form of audio tracking. It is actually based on visual reinforcement of the holes that are already present on the punched tape matrix. These holes in themselves represent the visual log of the note parameters, and the sequence therefore reflects a double transformation (from audio data to image data (real holes in the paper roll) and from image (punched tape matrix) to image (animation result)), so this work can nevertheless be regarded as audio tracking. In the last resort, however, the computer-assisted animation is based on the transfer of audio parameters to image parameters.

[334.mov/1–3] Stills from an audio-visual composition
[335] Extract from the audio wave form
[336] Horizontal cross-section through the centre of the animation
[337] Vertical cross-section through the centre of the animation
[338] Extract from the audio wave form
[339] Horizontal cross-section through the centre of the animation
[340] Vertical cross-section through the centre of the animation
[341] Extract from the audio wave form

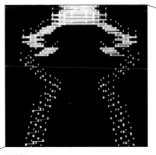

[335]

INFO [The graphical structure of the music score for a player piano is the basis of this animation, which has a structure and accentuation which are absolutely synchronic with the music because the music consists of these forms.]

These illustrations [336], [337] show the exact distribution of notes over time. Considering only one image line (in this case a horizontal line) makes the sequence of the composition visible. Individual notes are visualised by white dots. Their distribution and position determine the character of the composition. The vertical cross-section enables the playing time for individual notes to be visualised.

Stills [334.mov/2] from a composition based on the footage of a punched tape matrix for player pianos. The graphical structure is the visualisation of the sequence of notes.

[336] ›

[337] ›

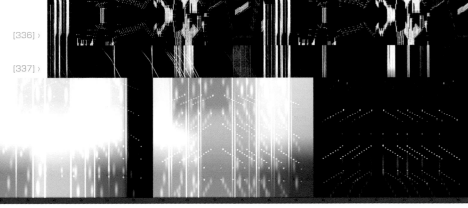

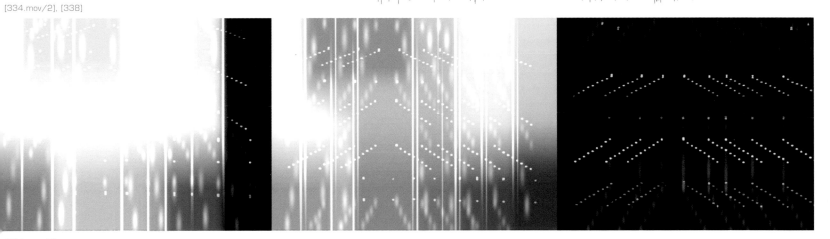

[334.mov/2], [338]

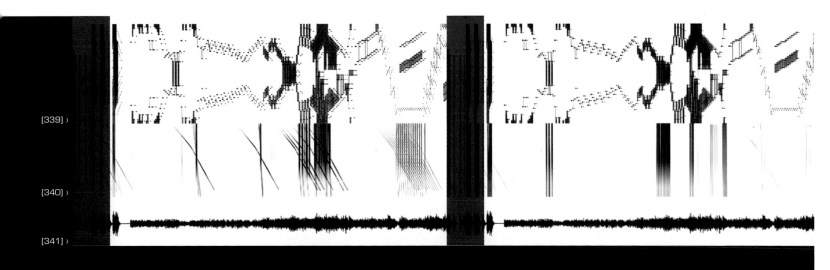

[334.mov/3]

[339] ›

[340] ›

[341] ›

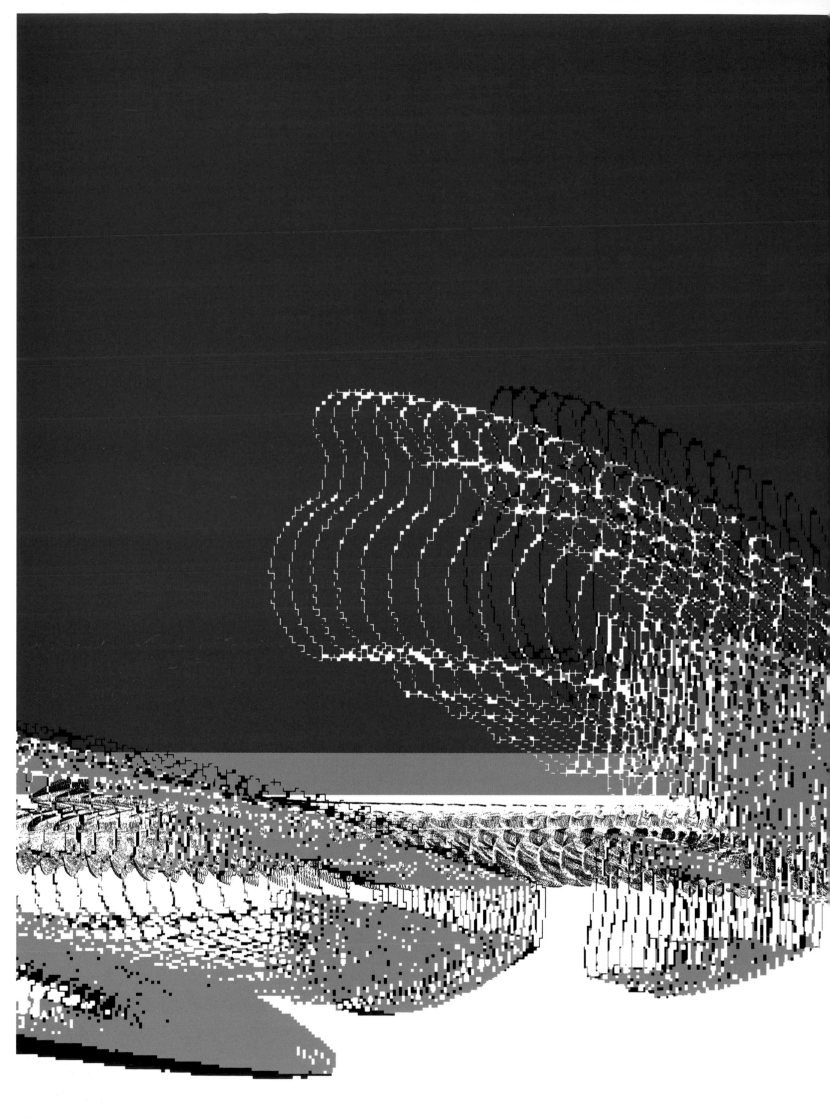

rules and behaviours

A very elegant way of developing grid systems for moving picture sequences is by determining the rules and behaviours to be assigned to objects and graphic elements. Following this principle, the designer who uses behaviours becomes a producer who determines the form and behaviour of his or her scene and the »actors«. Properties such as colour, shape, dynamics and the reactions of elements to their »environment« and their graphical »companions« can be defined.

By defining behaviours, the graphic objects are given a certain form of »minimal intelligence«. This tells them how to behave within what limits and under what conditions, which impulses they should react to and how they should react. The designer thus defines the rules of the interaction in the scene. With this mechanism, complex sequences can be created quickly from very simple »rules«, even without setting key frames.

Many particle effects are based on the definition of behaviours and not every object has to be animated individually. This not only applies to behaviours which simulate physical phenomena, behaviours can also be created by developing own sets of rules. This becomes interesting wherever the behaviour of objects is dynamically based on the behaviour of other objects, for example a delayed reaction to another object.

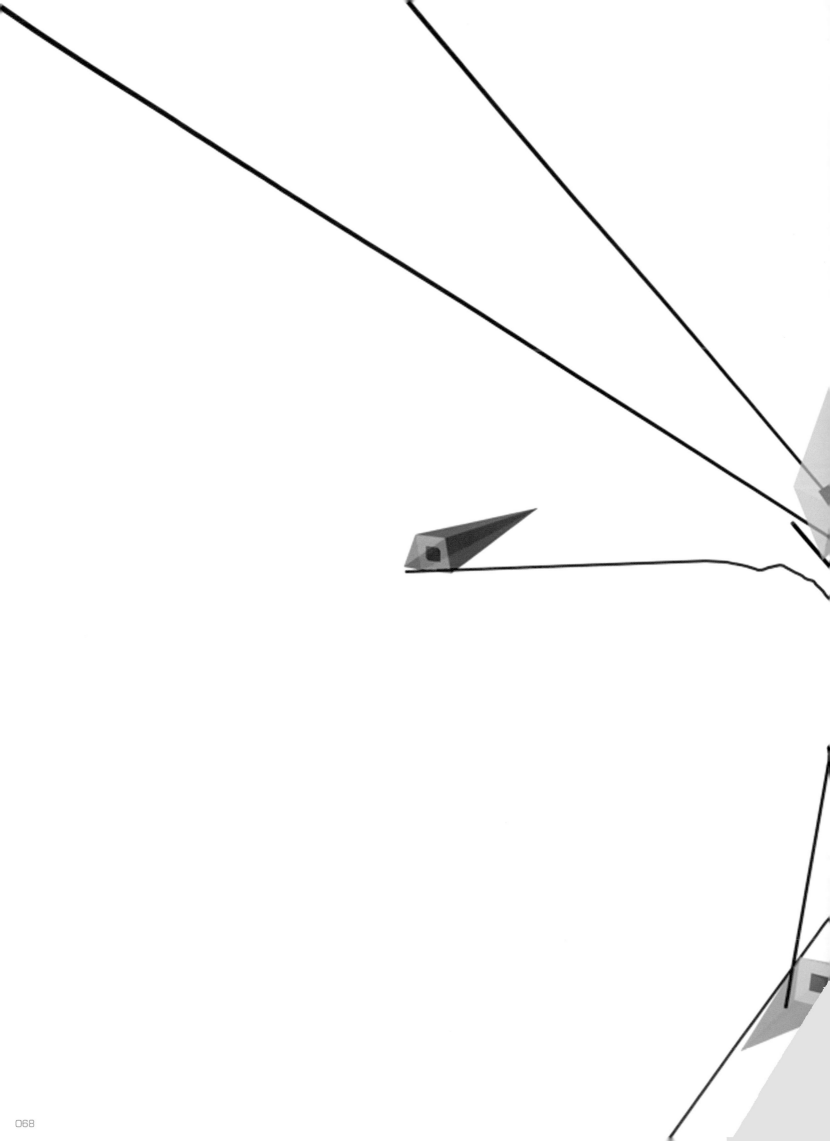

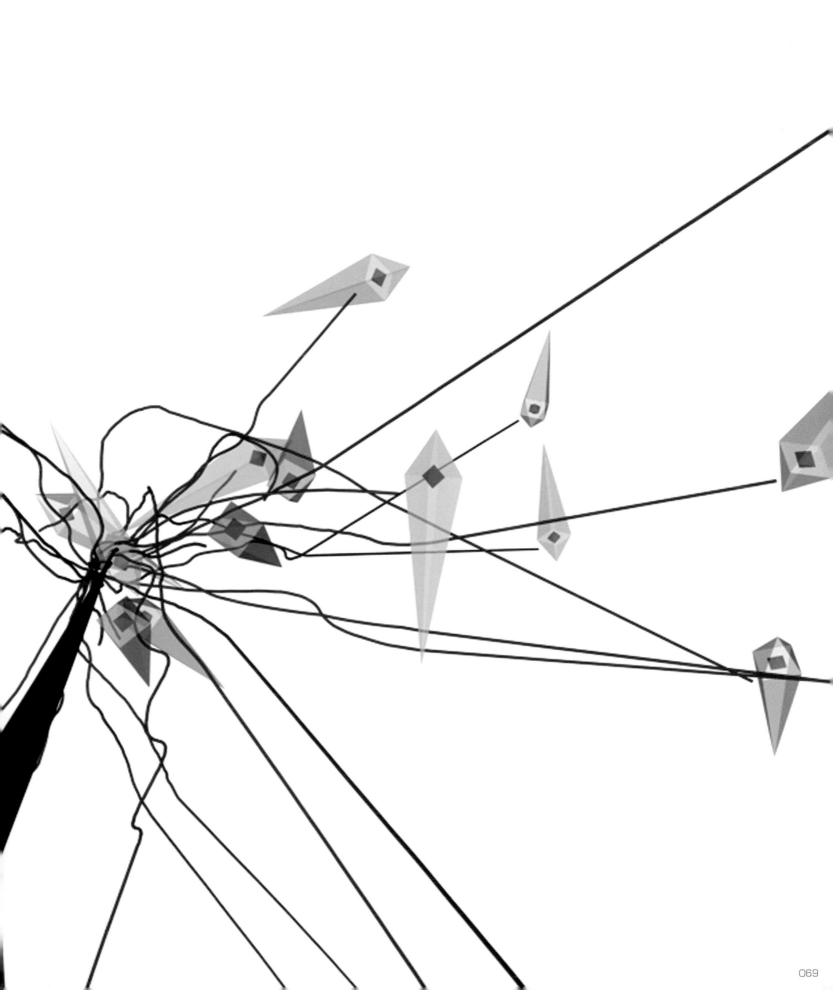

rules and behaviours

ORIENTATION >COLLISION >DISTORTION >SYNCHRONICITY >ATTRACTION >ALGORITHMS & PATTERN

Creating simple rules such as aligning objects to other objects provides a simple and effective grid
and might be the initial impulse for complex structures

GRID: 3D grid, 4D grid
PRINCIPLE: Using orientation and alignment of objects as grid
METHOD: Creating mass behaviour by aligning many objects to one
EXAMPLE: Motion graphic footage
CONTEXT: 016, 026, 050, 066, 124, 142
MOVIES: 401.mov, 402.mov

INFO [Simple rules, like aligning many objects to one, can easily create
effective mass behaviour and can often provide the impulse for powerful
scenes, especially when applied to large numbers of objects, as can be
seen in computer-animated films for cinema.]

[401.mov/1]

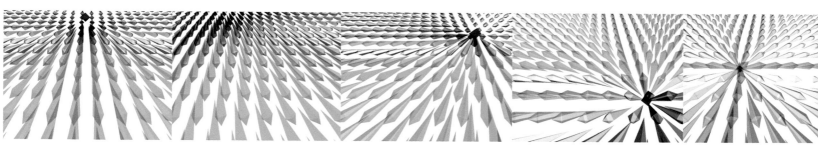

[401.mov/2-6]

alignment

Defining simple »follow me« behaviours for individual objects or several objects can quickly and easily
generate dramatic sequences. The linking of elements or their behaviour is also a good method to create
a dramaturgy quickly. It is defined as how B should react when A acts; like in programming, a sequence
»if... then...« is defined.

As can be seen in this example [401.mov/2-6], all grey objects are aligned with their tips pointing to the
red object. They do not move from their geographical position, they merely change their alignment. The
impulse to do this comes from the red octahedron, which in turn carries out movements in space with its
defined behaviour.

[402.mov/1]

The grey objects change their position according to the red octahedron, so when it moves they follow it and always align their tips towards it.

TIP [A slight delay or inaccuracy in the combination of the leading and following object makes the animation seem very lively.]

[402.mov/2]

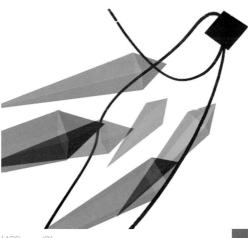

[402.mov/3]

[402.mov/4]

[402.mov/5]

The red path shows the dynamics and the sequence of movements of the red object.

The grey objects follow with a slight delay. This creates the subjective impression of watching a stylised living being.

[402.mov/6–7]

[402.mov/8] ›

By different settings of the behaviour parameters, an attractive inaccuracy can be defined in the reactions of the grey elements to the movements of the octahedron. Depending on how quickly and with what accuracy the grey objects react to the behaviour of the octahedron, the impression arises that the objects have a certain degree of independence.

[401.mov/1–6] Stills from a behaviour-controlled sequence
[402.mov/1–8] Stills and sequences from a behaviour-controlled sequence

rules and behaviours

>ORIENTATION COLLISION >DISTORTION >SYNCHRONICITY >ATTRACTION ALGORITHMS & PATTERN

The simulation of numerous physical principles can be used as a basis and
a grid for moving image sequences

GRID: 3D grid, 4D grid
PRINCIPLE: Using gravity of relating objects as grid
METHOD: Defining alignment and tracing
EXAMPLE: Gravitation of virtual planets
CONTEXT: 016, 050, 066, 133, 142
MOVIE: 410.mov

[403]

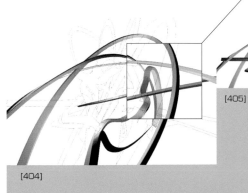

[404]

[405]   [406]   [407]   [408]

Each of these pictures highlights
a different movement path of a
sphere.

[403] Movement paths of all spheres
[404] Highlighting the movement path: sphere 1
[405] Movement paths of all spheres and sphere 2
[406] Highlighting the movement path: sphere 2
[407] Movement paths of all spheres and sphere 3
[408] Highlighting the movement path: sphere 3
[409] Movement paths of all spheres, situation 1
[410.mov/1] Still from the animation
[410.mov/2] Sequence from the animation
[411] Movement paths of all spheres, situation 2
[410.mov/3] Sequence from the animation

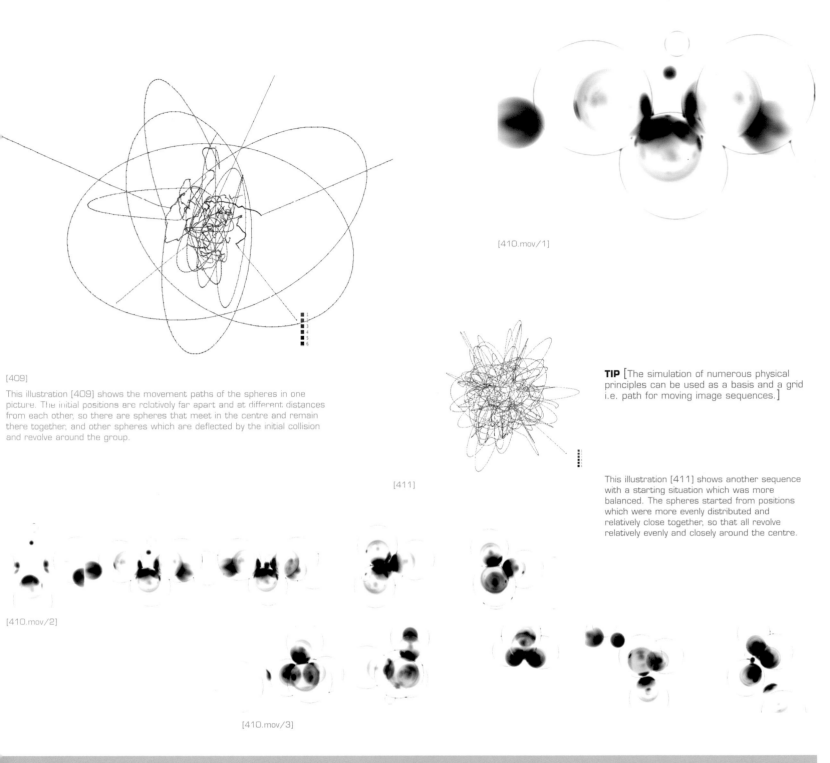

[410.mov/1]

[409]

This illustration [409] shows the movement paths of the spheres in one picture. The initial positions are relatively far apart and at different distances from each other, so there are spheres that meet in the centre and remain there together, and other spheres which are deflected by the initial collision and revolve around the group.

TIP [The simulation of numerous physical principles can be used as a basis and a grid i.e. path for moving image sequences.]

[411]

This illustration [411] shows another sequence with a starting situation which was more balanced. The spheres started from positions which were more evenly distributed and relatively close together, so that all revolve relatively evenly and closely around the centre.

[410.mov/2]

[410.mov/3]

collision

This sequence is based on the simulation of behaviour derived from physics. Each object is assigned a force of attraction – a gravitation value. This force affects other objects. At the beginning of the animation all the spheres are at different distances from each other, so they develop different speeds during the sequence before they collide in the centre. The basic behaviour of moving towards each other is caused by the gravitation effect which each sphere has on every other sphere. The distance between the spheres therefore means that the gravitation of each sphere has different effects on others, and generates greater or lesser speeds amongst the spheres. Some collide in the centre, thus causing new and complex movement sequences of the affected spheres. As in billiards, they then change their paths and rotate or become slower or faster. Others fly past the group and are only drawn back after some time by the gravitation of the spheres in the centre.

The fact that a large number of objects affect each other and that their speed, movement, direction and dynamics depend on the behaviour of other objects leads to a situation which is difficult to predict. That is exactly where the attraction lies – it is no longer possible to predetermine everything; the defined parameters and object characteristics themselves generate an independent dynamic effect in the sequence. Very different visual solutions can result from these procedures. Only the fundamental underlying principle is shown here.

rules and behaviours

>ORIENTATION >COLLISION **DISTORTION** >SYNCHRONICITY >ATTRACTION >ALGORITHMS & PATTERN

Defining the material composition and fixing gravitation point outside the object leads to the behaviour in this animation

[412]

[413]

The distortions of the surface are caused by a virtual gravitation point on the left of the screen. The material characteristics assigned to the object reinforce this effect, it is relatively slow to react.

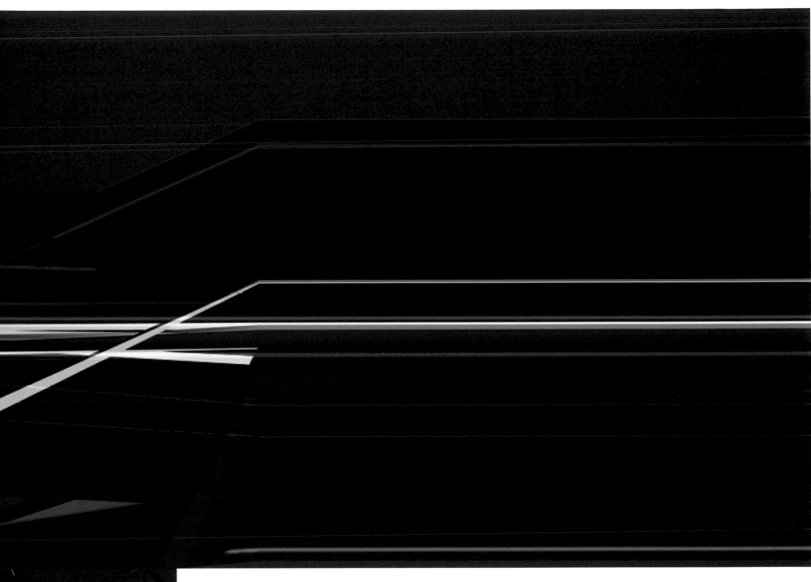

RULE [The longer the object is subjected to gravitation, the greater are the distortions.]

distortion

This sequence results from physical behaviour which is essentially based on gravitation. A three-dimensional object has been created, and by adding properties and reactions it has acquired its own behaviour. This not only results from the defined behaviour of the object; its material composition and the courseness of its structure also play a role. They cause a certain inertia in the reaction of the object to outside influences and lead to an angular distortion of its surface.

In this specific example, a gravitation point has been placed on the left of the screen which has an effect on the object. Forces act upon each other both inside and outside the surface, and eventually they cause the distortion of the surface. The distortion of the object is caused by a virtual gravitation point on the left side of the screen. The effect is made even stronger by the material properties assigned to the object – it is relatively inert.

[412] Still and sequence from the animation
[413] Illustration of the 3D structure in its distorted condition

rules and behaviours

>ORIENTATION >COLLISION DISTORTION >SYNCHRONICITY >ATTRACTION >ALGORITHMS & PATTERN

Defining the material composition and fixing gravitation points outside the object leads to the behaviour in this animation

GRID: 3D grid, 4D grid
PRINCIPLE: Using gravity in the surroundings as grid
METHOD: Defining material and gravitation
EXAMPLE: Motion graphics footage
CONTEXT: 034, 038, 066, 124, 148
MOVIE: –

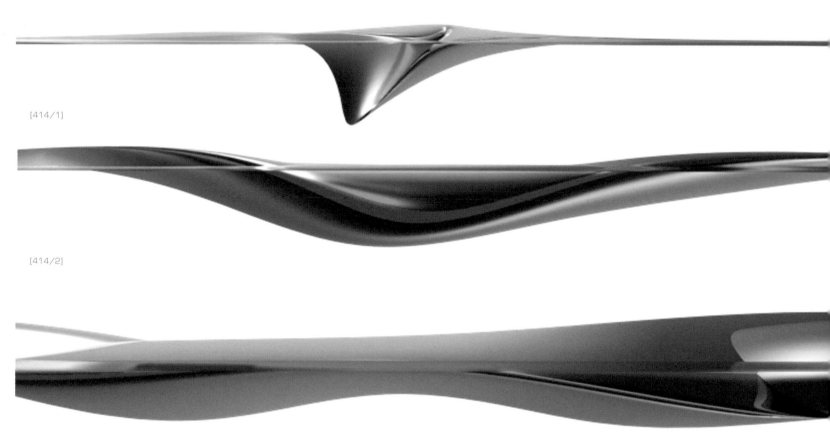

[414/1]

[414/2]

[414/3]

RULE [The distortions of the surface are caused by a virtual gravitation point in space.]

[414/1–3] Stills of the animation
[415] Structure of a dynamic 3D object
[416] Dynamic 3D object as basic element for an image design
[417/1–3] Stills of the animation

gravitation and inertia

This sequence also results from physical behaviour. It is also based on gravitation. As a result of the fine detail in the design of the 3D objects, an exact and differentiated reaction of the objects to the gravitation point in the space can be observed. They distort much more elegantly than the example on the previous page. This shows the effect which the characteristics of the material and the resolution of the design of the object have on the appearance and progress of the sequence.

Precise interventions in the dynamics of the behaviour can quickly create interesting, automatically generated, visually dramatic effects. The behaviour of the object more or less provides the spatial and temporal »grid« for the animation, depending on the individual intervention. Creating individual key frames is not necessary. Instead, the designer spends his time defining the appropriate parameters.

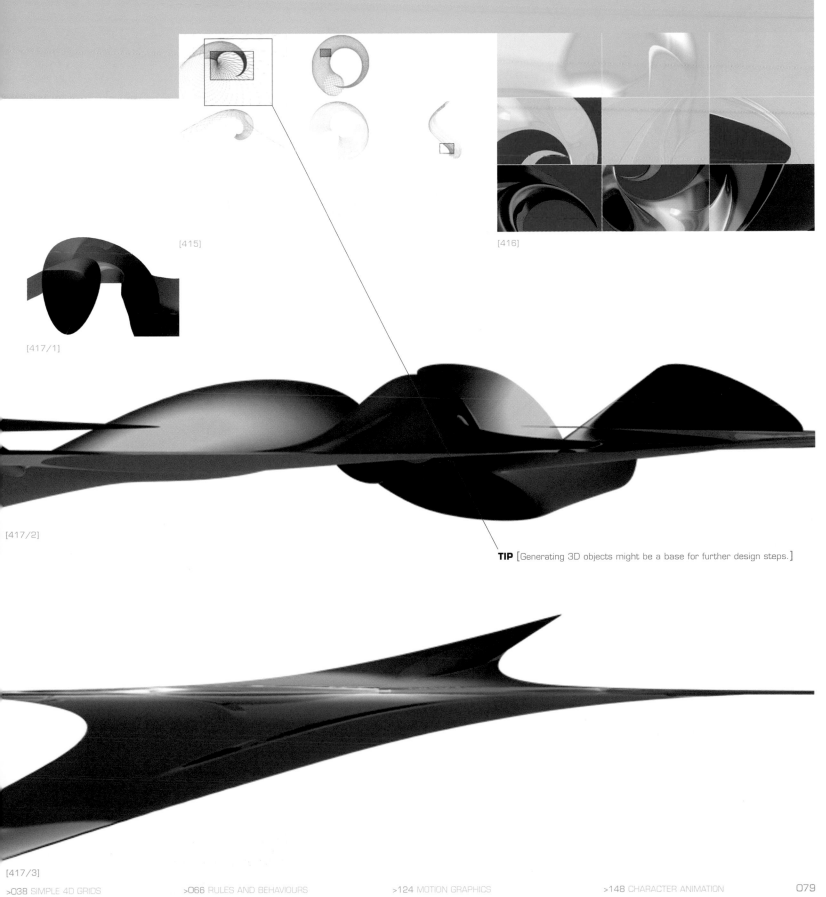

[415]

[416]

[417/1]

[417/2]

TIP [Generating 3D objects might be a base for further design steps.]

[417/3]

rules and behaviours

>ORIENTATION >COLLISION **DISTORTION** >SYNCHRONICITY >ATTRACTION >ALGORITHMS & PATTERN

Behaviours which are assigned to the design of objects can cause changes to objects
during the animation and thus determine their grid

GRID: 3D grid, 4D grid
PRINCIPLE: Using object gravity as grid
METHOD: Defining gravitation within an object
EXAMPLE: Motion graphic footage
CONTEXT: 016, 034, 038, 066
MOVIE: 418.mov

RULE [Gravitation within the object causes object
distortion, sometimes until a new object arises.]

[418.mov/1–6]

rules and behaviours

>ORIENTATION >COLLISION **DISTORTION** >SYNCHRONICITY >ATTRACTION >ALGORITHMS & PATTERN

GRID: 3D grid, 4D grid
PRINCIPLE: Using object gravity as grid
METHOD: Defining gravitation within an object
EXAMPLE: Motion graphic footage

gravitation within objects

This animation, like the previous animations, is fundamentally based on principles derived from physics. In this example, however, the forces only act within the 3D object. The remaining space around the object is not affected by them. The changes to the object were determined by appropriate settings in the pre-defined behavioural plug-in of a 3D program. Manual creation of key frames is no longer necessary – the behaviour is a hundred per cent relevant as a grid for the temporal and spatial change in the object.

[419/1]

[419/2]

This illustration [419] shows at what points on the object gravitation forces were applied, and along which paths they act on each other. When gravitation is activated, the object begins to contract until it eventually collapses and a completely new object arises.

[419/3]

[418.mov/7]

[418.mov/8]

[418.mov/9]

[418.mov/1–6] Stills from the animation
[419/1–3] Stills and sequence of the 3D structure
[418.mov/7–9] Stills and sequence from the animation

rules and behaviours

>ORIENTATION >COLLISION >DISTORTION SYNCHRONICITY >ATTRACTION >ALGORITHMS & PATTERN

Grids which are based on combinations and temporal matching of graphical elements have a decisive
effect on the elegant appearance of sequences

GRID: 4D grid
PRINCIPLE: Using orientation of graphical elements as grid
METHOD: Temporal matching of element movement
EXAMPLE: Motion graphic footage
CONTEXT: 016, 038, 050, 066
MOVIE: –

[420/1–6]

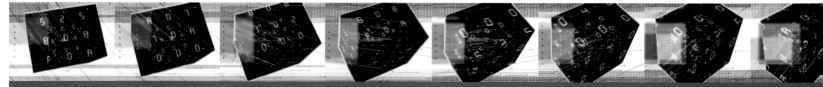

synchronicity

This animation works with behaviours which are very freely formulated and in some cases manually created. This means that, unlike the previous examples, automatisms and parametric changes were not used – a key frame-based combination and reaction of design elements was used instead. Few elements are directly linked to each other. For example, the angle of the small »needles« follows the movement of the rectangles.

In spite of the small number of direct links, the individual graphical elements still seem to be in contact with each other. This smooth and elegant effect is essentially due to the movement direction and the timing, which is constantly synchronised between the graphical elements. For example, individual elements form a temporary group because they move in the same direction with the same speed. In this way, a relatively great effect has been created here with relatively small means.

This animation is a good example of the fact that no automation or grid can replace the virtuosity of the designer. A sense of dynamics and dramaturgy is necessary even when the best grid systems are used, because they are merely tools to create or adhere to visual rules.

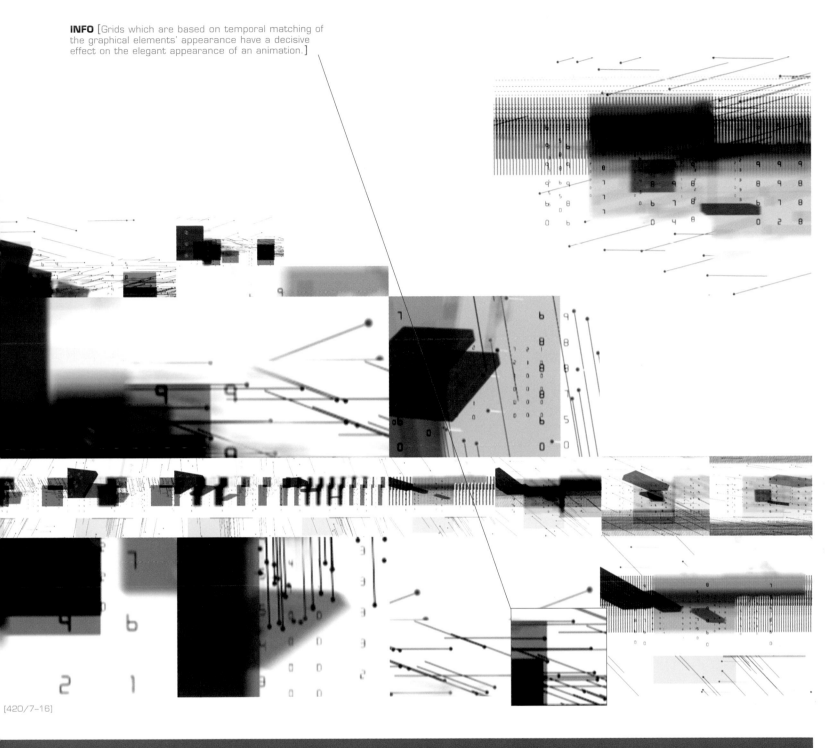

INFO [Grids which are based on temporal matching of the graphical elements' appearance have a decisive effect on the elegant appearance of an animation.]

[420/7–16]

[420/1–16] Stills and sequences from the animation

rules and behaviours

>ORIENTATION >COLLISION >DISTORTION >SYNCHRONICITY ATTRACTION >ALGORITHMS & PATTERN

Time grids such as sequential arrangements of motifs can have strong visual effects
The dynamic alignment of the behaviour of one or more objects is related to the dynamics of another object

GRID: 3D grid, 4D grid
PRINCIPLE: Using attraction of objects as grid
METHOD: Sequential arrangement, alignment
EXAMPLE: Motion graphic footage
CONTEXT: 016, 066, 126, 142
MOVIE: –

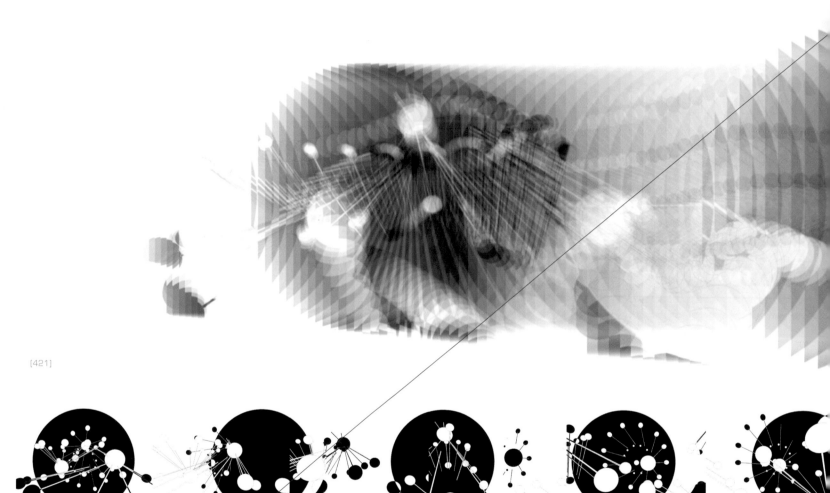

[421]

[422/1]

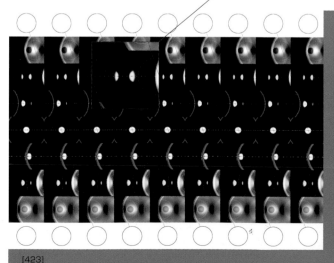

[423]

This sequence shows in visible form how the circles move over time from left to right (time moves from top to bottom in the illustration). Here, the exact part which has already left the picture on the right is shown again on the left of the picture. In this way a sequential arrangement of several videos is possible, that together create the impression of a large animation.

[421] Display of the sequence in one image
[422/1] Sequence from the animation
[423] Sequential build-up and layout of an animation
[422/2] Sequential build-up and layout of an animation with horizontal offset

INFO [In this sequence, the exact part of the circle which has already left the picture on the right is shown again on the left of the picture.]

[422/2]

In this sequence, the original position of the circle has been marked as a reference point. This shows how the circle moves from left to right over time. Here again, the part of the circle that is no longer visible on the right of the screen enters the picture again on the left.

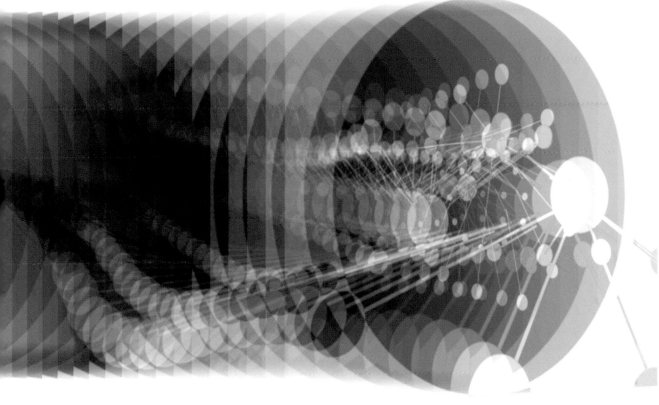

This illustration shows the sequence of the animation in one picture. The different movement forms and frequencies of the small spheres are clearly visible. They are sometimes closer to the centre or the other small spheres, sometimes further away.

dynamic gravitation and sequential arrangement

This animation is interesting in two respects. On the one hand it shows how sequential structures work when in a tiled form, and on the other hand it shows how graphical objects can be visually linked by manually defined behaviours. The smaller spheres always follow the slightly larger spheres in the centre. At the same time they move from right to left across the screen. Due to the pre-defined behaviour, the dynamics of the smaller spheres over time mean that they are sometimes closer to the centre and the large sphere, and sometimes further away. The »rods« fixed to the smaller spheres are always aligned towards the sphere in the centre. This means that the difference in distance, and thus the inertia and dynamics of the smaller spheres, can be clearly seen.

Another interesting aspect of this animation is its potential for sequential arrangement. With little distance between the projection devices, this animation appears to be a continuous sequence. The large sphere in the middle moves off the screen to the right with a frequency which is slightly offset against the frequency with which it appears again on the left. This means that linking animations together makes it possible to create the impression of a single large sequence.

rules and behaviours

>ORIENTATION >COLLISION >DISTORTION >SYNCHRONICITY >ATTRACTION ALGORITHM & PATTERN

The analysis, as well as generation of visual patterns can form a basis for the creation of grids for moving image sequences

GRID: 3D grid, 4D grid
PRINCIPLE: Using visual patterns or algorithms as grid
METHOD: Analysing and generation of visual or mathematical rules
EXAMPLE: Visuals used as grid or shading
CONTEXT: 024, 046, 066, 088, 134
MOVIES: 427.mov, 428.mov, 431.mov

‹ [424/1-5]
‹ [425/1-5]   [424/5]

[424/4]   [426/1-4]   [425/5]

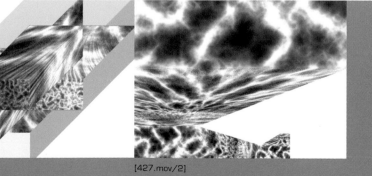

[427.mov/1]   [427.mov/2]

[424/1–5] Various volume shadings with black-and-white pattern
[425/1–5] Various volume shadings with colour pattern
[426/1–4] Construction of a partially fractal geometric object
[424/4] Result of a volume shading
[427.mov/1–2] Volumetric display of a fractal time sequence
[428.mov/1–2] Zoom stages of a black-and-white pattern
[429] Zoom stages of a black-and-white pattern
[430/1–2] Zoom stages of a structure
[431.mov] Sequence of changes to an object

[429]

View of various zoom stages in a visual
grid that is based on the repetition of
similar elements.

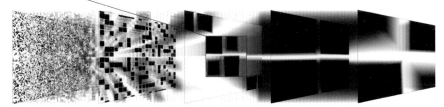

[428.mov/1]

A space-time cross-section of the sequence
[429.mov/1] shows that the visual structure
of the animation is repeated throughout a
period of time, in all aspects, i.e. in the detail
as well as the bigger picture.

[428.mov/2]

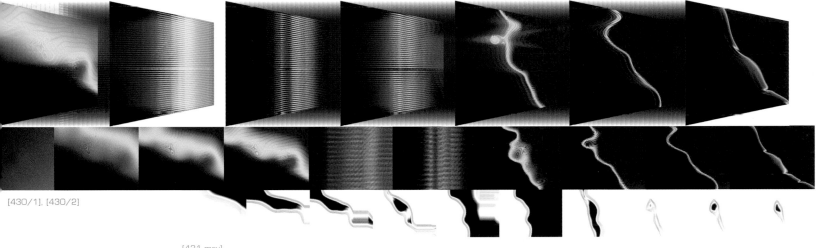

[430/1]. [430/2]

[431.mov]

TIP [Both the analysing and generating of visual patterns is
a basis for the design of grids for moving image sequences.]

algorithm and patterns

A central technique in digital moving image design is working with algorithms, i.e. with rules in the mathematical sense –
and after all, that is what behaviours are too. Here, however, it concerns the rules manifested visually in a still or
sequence. This can be the result, the origin or the method of the creative work. Simple rules like the repetition of
graphical elements and patterns offer a wide range of possibilities for use. For example, micro views and macro views can
be generated or structures created which not only have fractal forms, but which also show fractal behaviours over a long
period.

Complex links and relationships which exist between the graphical elements or film motifs used within single pictures or
image sequences can provide a good basis for grids. They represent a manifestation of principles at a specific time which
has an effect on the elements of a picture over a certain period or at a particular time – like a picture of a river which
shows the passage of time by its course (or like movement which fundamentally becomes visible in the form of growth etc.).

Hence it is possible to take any motif and derive principles which are visible merely by the manifestation of the visual
relationships in just one image. Parameter transfer in the form of multiple tracking or displacing can be used to extract
the complete set of relationships which exist between graphical elements and transfer it to other elements. In principle
this is a complete grid transfer from one set of graphical elements to another.

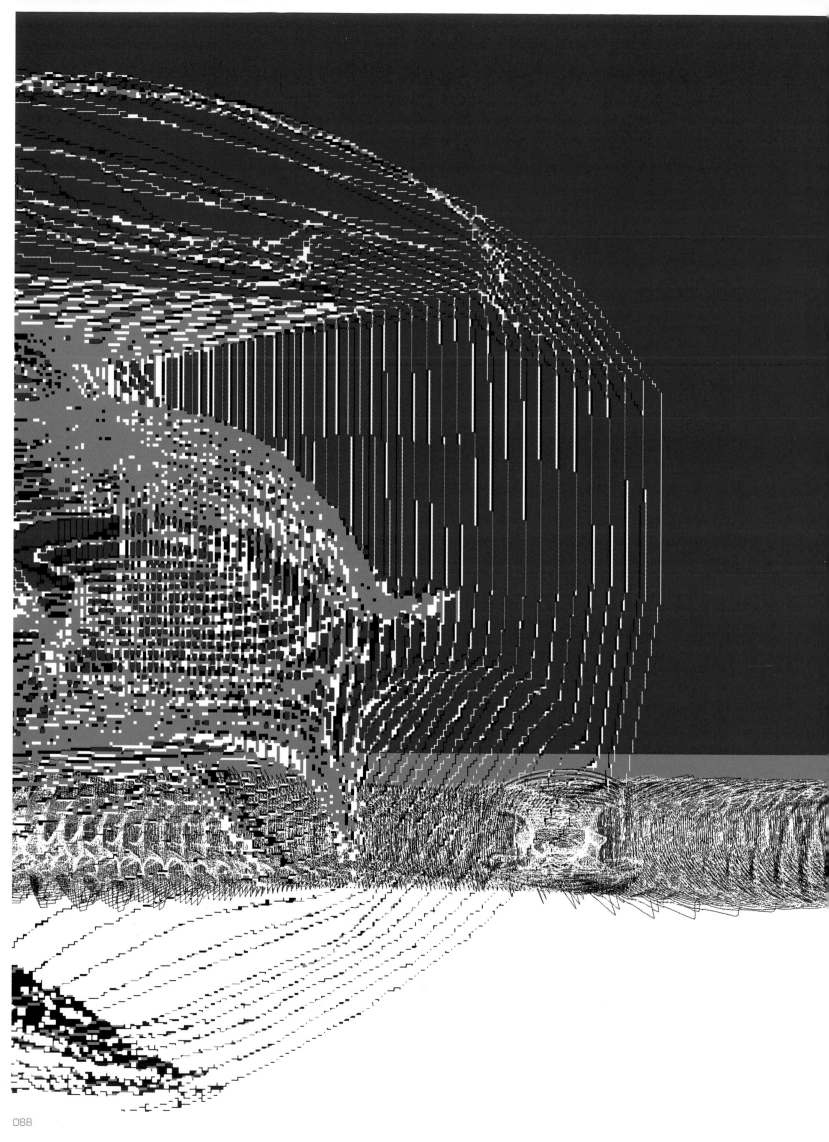

displacing
displacing

Displacing is a method that is often used in the design of moving image sequences. This method can, if applied universally, function as a template to steer the graphic elements of a whole animation. It can have such a dominant effect on the action in animations that it is presented here in great detail as a grid for moving image sequences. Displacing is equally simple a principle as it is powerful to generate dramaturgies quickly and efficiently.

The values of properties of graphical elements such as brightness, colour or saturation are analysed and transferred to other parameters of the same element or other elements. In this way, models for the appearance and behaviour of graphical elements can be quickly generated. The model or motif from which the values are derived and transferred is normally not a visible part of the animation, rather a specifically created element (grid); a displacement map.

The fundamental idea is to analyse the principles contained in the properties or in the change of a displacement map and use the gained »dramaturgy« as a grid for other elements. Brightness values of a displacement map can in this way also determine the spatial and temporal behaviour, i.e. steer a movement.

displacing

The luminance value of an element/layer can be used as an impulse to control other elements or layers

GRID: 3D grid, 4D grid
PRINCIPLE: Using luminance value as a grid
METHOD: Displacing size of typography
EXAMPLE: Typographic animation
CONTEXT: 016, 048, 088, 156
MOVIE: –

INFO [Displacement maps which transfer luminance values into the third dimension are called »bump maps«.]

[501]

A motif with an unsharp bright circle in the centre is the displacement map for the first result, the raised section in the flat surface. The 8-bit greyscale values were transferred to the third dimension (bump map). Thus, bright pixels create a greater height. In the next step this image was mapped to a sphere.

This image shows the principle of displacement very clearly. The values for the brightness of an object can determine the values for other properties of the object. In the first phase, the transfer of the brightness values leads to the three-dimensional raising of the object.

The motif [502] with the red dots is the displacement map, the grid for the typographic animation. The luminance value in the grid animation has been directly linked with the size of the letters in the visible image track. The display of the luminance values in the form of a graph shows the mathematical connection between the brightness value and the letter size.

[502]

displacing

Transferring the luminance values of a graphical element to the values of visual properties of other elements is a frequently used method to coordinate design elements in animations and visually link them to each other. This principle is really a form of property tracking. This method can be so striking that it can be used as a fundamental grid principle for moving image sequences. The brightness value is often the impulse which controls another parameter. If the luminance values in the element analysed are changed outside the animation, this also leads to a corresponding change in the values linked to this element. For example, if the luminance values of a pattern are linked with the size of another graphical element, the size of the element changes in accordance with the changes in the luminance values of the pattern. The element becomes smaller or larger.

The parametric transfer of grid values to image layers is not always carried out directly. For example, there is often a spatial or temporal shift between the changes in the grid and the changes in the visible image element. This is an indirect link between the displacement map and the layer.

[503/1]   [503/2]   [503/3]   [503/4]   [503/5]

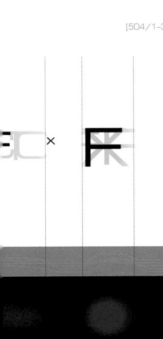

[504/1-3] ›

[504/4]   [504/5]   [504/6]

The luminance values in the lower row of pictures determine the number
and size of the typographical particles generated, with a ratio of 1:1.
The grid is almost a sort of template. As a result, the design of the grid
and the changes in its parameters change the connected parameters of
the image layer.

[505]

RULE [The brighter the values of the grid (red), the larger
the number and size of the letters or particles generated
in the same positions.]

[506]

[501] Illustration of various displacement steps
[502] The connection between displacement graphics and type size
[503/1-5] Stills from typographic animation 1
[504/1-6] Stills from typographic animation 2 and their displacement map
[505] Illustration generated by displacement
[506] 8-bit greyscale display of the displacement map [502]

displacing

>SIZE **VOLUME** >POSITION >TIME

Displacement can be used to generate the three-dimensional appearance of objects/layers

GRID: 3D grid, 4D grid
PRINCIPLE: Using brightness value as a grid
METHOD: Displacing volume
EXAMPLE: Typographic animation
CONTEXT: 034, 048, 088, 158
MOVIE: 507.mov

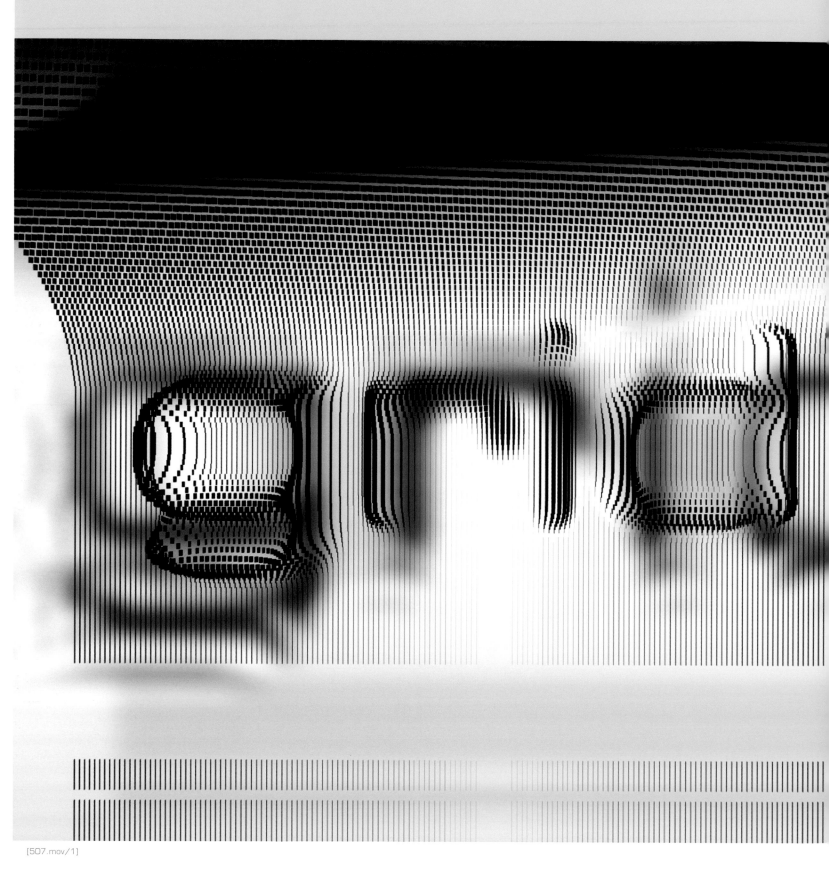

[507.mov/1]

INFO [The background motif is used as a »bump map«.]

interface

[507.mov/2–6]

[507.mov/7–13]

volume
The brightness values of the background design in this animation have caused the three-dimensional shift of the motif in the foreground.

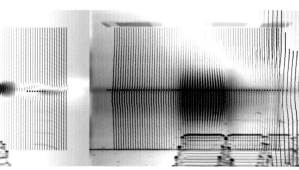

[507.mov/14]   [507.mov/15]

[507.mov/1–15] Various stills from an animation based on displacement

displacing

Displacement can be used to generate dynamic changes of object positions

GRID: 2D grid, 4D grid
PRINCIPLE: Using brightness and audio value as a grid
METHOD: Displacing position
EXAMPLE: Audio-visual animation for a stage
CONTEXT: 048, 062, 088, 158
MOVIE: 508.mov

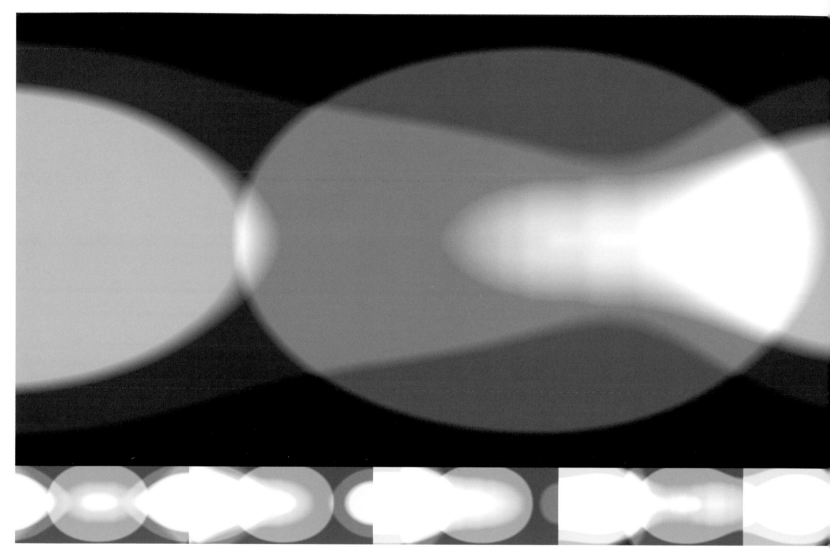

[508.mov/1-2]

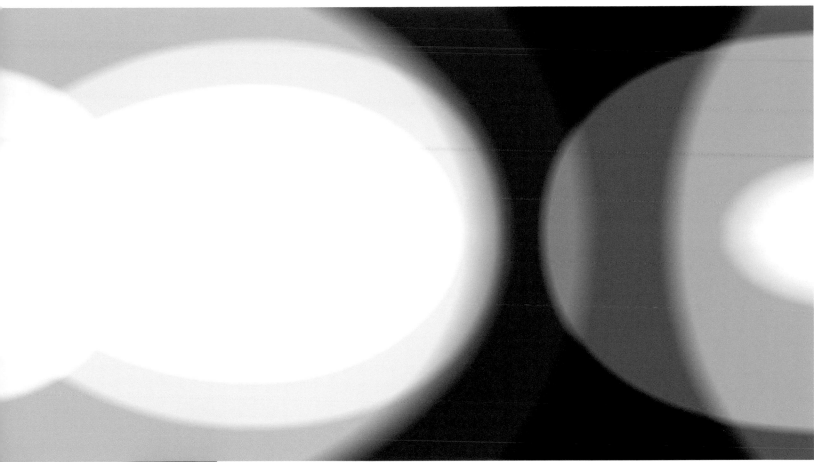

[508.mov/3]

The graphics in this animation have been animated automatically by displacement. There was also a direct link with the sound so that this animation is absolutely synchronous in its dynamic with the audio track.

[508.mov/1–3] Stills and sequence from an animation based on displacement and audio tracking

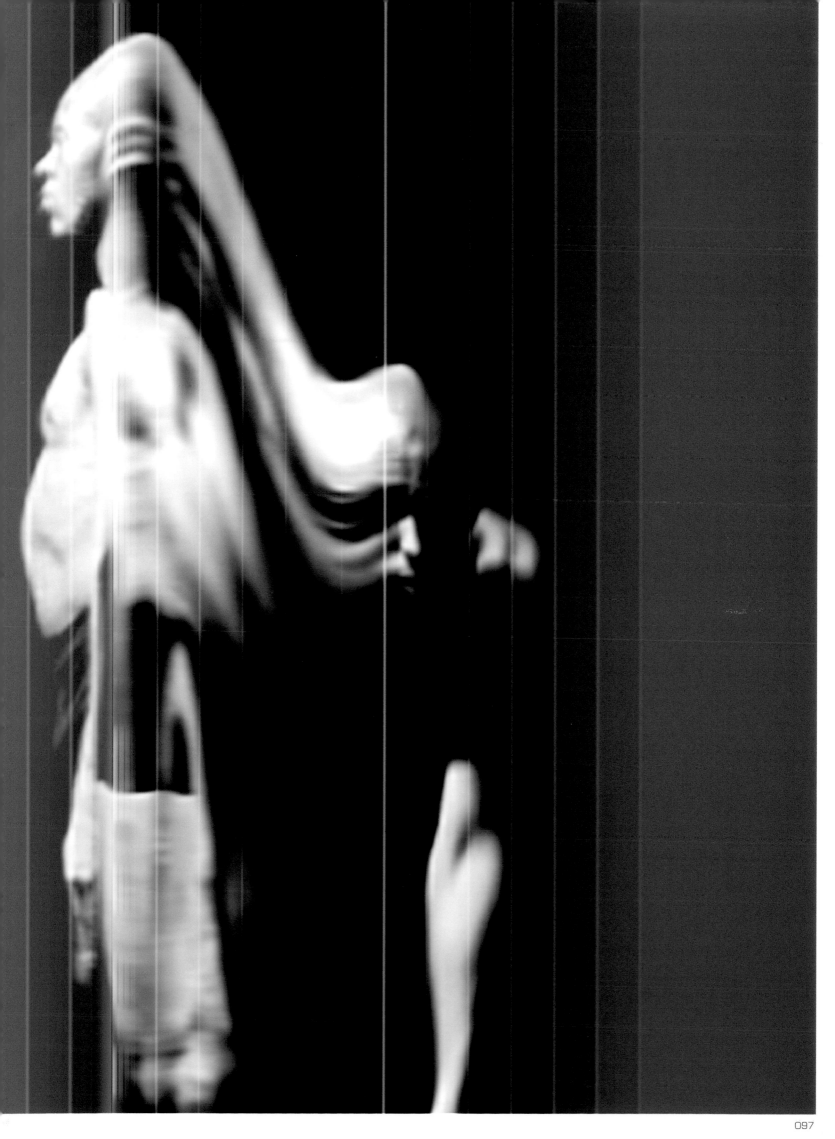

displacing

>SIZE >VOLUME >POSITION TIME

Displacement can be used as a model for the manipulation of time sequences

GRID: 2D grid, 4D grid
PRINCIPLE: Using luminance and audio values as a grid
METHOD: Displacing time
EXAMPLE: Audio-visual composition for a dance theatre performance
CONTEXT: 018, 042, 044, 088
MOVIE: 509.mov

[509.mov/1]   [509.mov/2]   [509.mov/3]

dance theater
These animations were created for a dance theatre performance which dealt with the subject of time.
They are mainly based on the manipulation of temporal relationships in the sequences and the associated
output. In addition to the timing, the 4D grids that were generated also influenced the visual appearance
of the sequences. The visuals directly manifest the effects of the 4D grid in their formal appearance. A
number of variants of time displacement and tracking were used in the framework of the project. The
following examples show that even very simple displacement maps can be used in a wide variety of ways,
and that fascinating pictures can be generated in this way.

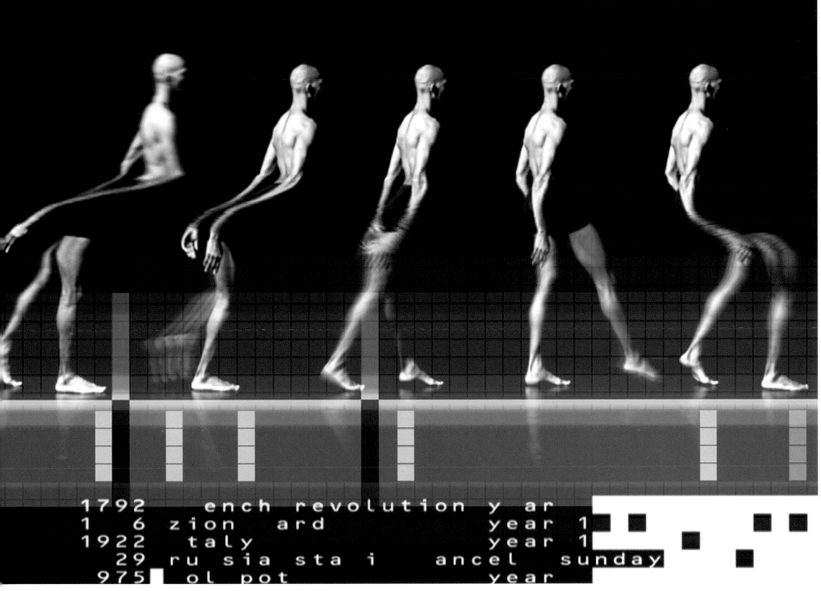

1792   ench revolution y ar
1 6 zion   ard   year 1
1922   taly   year 1
  29 ru sia sta i   ancel   sunday
 975 ol pot   year

[509.mov/4]

[509.mov/1–4] Stills from an animation based on displacement

displacing

>SIZE >VOLUME >POSITION TIME

Grid sequences from the original footage applied to the same footage as the final sequence

GRID: 2D grid, 4D grid
PRINCIPLE: Using luminance and audio values as a grid
METHOD: Displacing time
EXAMPLE: Audio-visual composition for a dance theatre performance
CONTEXT: 018, 042, 044, 088
MOVIE: 510.mov

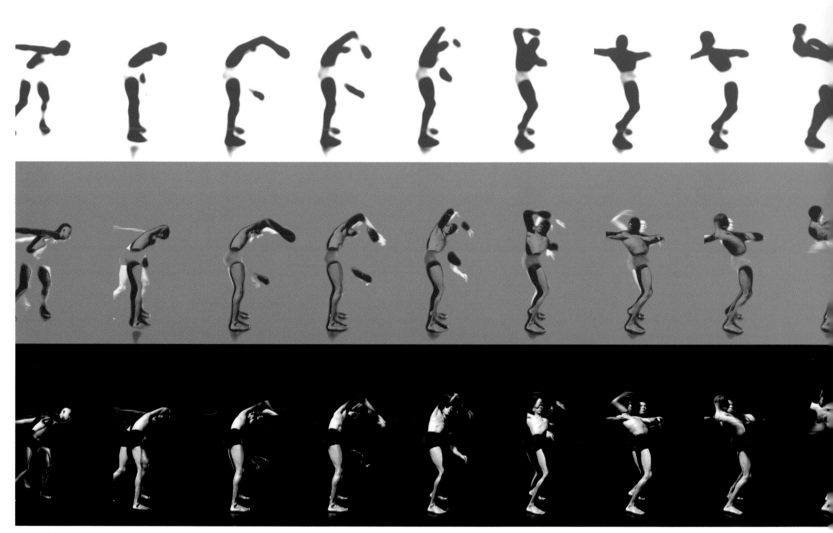

[511], [512], [513]

time displacement

The grid that is used here was derived from the same footage as the final sequence – from video material of the dance rehearsals. The material for the grid was then distorted, slightly abstracted and softened. Then the luminance values of the grid sequence were transferred to the luminance values of pictures from the real footage. Wherever the distorted material of the grid was coloured, the original footage became more or less visible depending on the brightness. The pictures of the sequence show a sequence of the original footage with an activated grid. This not only determines the visibility of the original footage, but also its behaviour over time.

In addition to the pure luminance displacement, pictures from subsequent frames were also faded into the currently visible picture. That means that the grid was used, first of all, to add a second motif in keeping with the brightness of the grid in the places where the colour of the grid is visible. Secondly, it was determined that this added motif would be generated from the future, i.e. a few frames later. The overlapping of the present and the future is thus visible in a motif in the current frame.

RULE [The darker the colour, the more clearly the motif of the original is visible.]

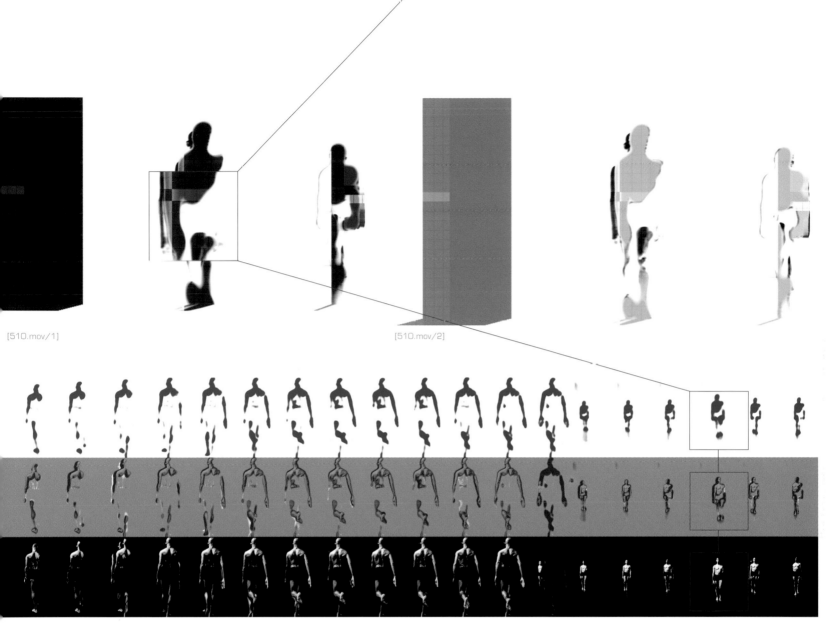

[510.mov/1]

[510.mov/2]

[514], [515], [516]

[510.mov/3]

The grid of this sequence was also taken from the original footage, and at the same time affects this footage. In the example on the left, a motif from the future has been faded in over the current frame. The original footage and the footage with a grid are faded in over each other with stroboscopic effects.

[511] Displacement map
[512] Displacement map and real footage
[513] Sequence from the animation
[510.mov/1–2] Stills from the animation
[514] Displacement map
[515] Displacement map and real footage
[516] Sequence from the animation
[510.mov/3] Sequence from the animation

displacing

>SIZE >VOLUME >POSITION TIME

Displacement maps can be used as a dynamic grid to control visual and temporal effects

GRID: 2D grid, 4D grid
PRINCIPLE: Using luminance and audio values as a grid
METHOD: Displacing time
EXAMPLE: Audio-visual composition for a dance theatre performance
CONTEXT: 018, 042, 044, 088
MOVIE: 510.mov

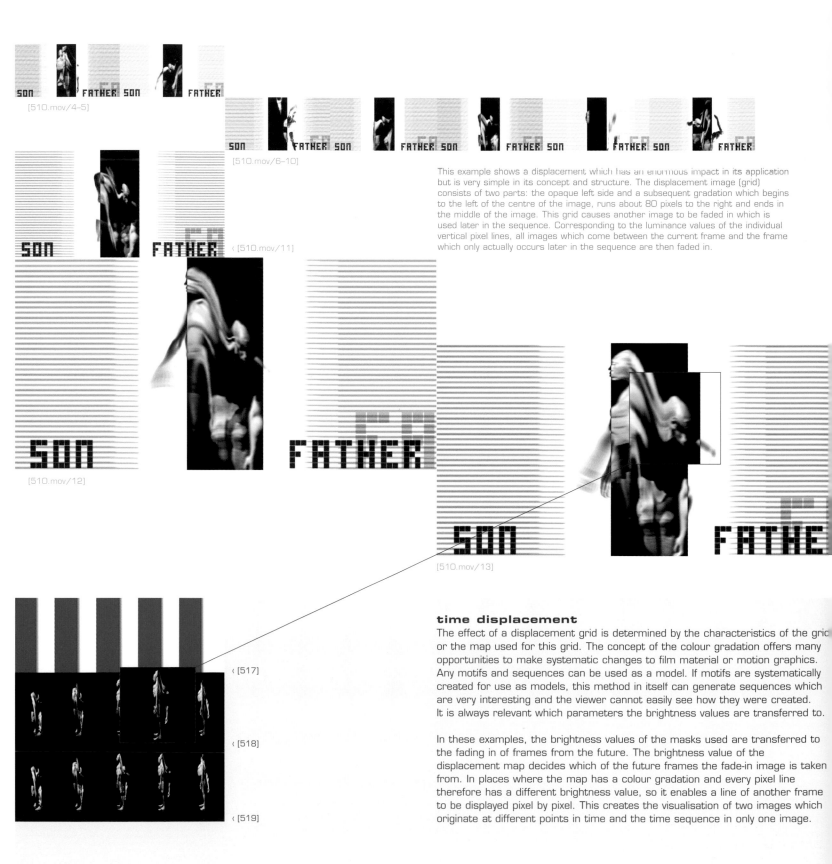

[510.mov/4-5]

[510.mov/6-10]

‹ [510.mov/11]

[510.mov/12]

[510.mov/13]

‹ [517]

‹ [518]

‹ [519]

This example shows a displacement which has an enormous impact in its application but is very simple in its concept and structure. The displacement image (grid) consists of two parts: the opaque left side and a subsequent gradation which begins to the left of the centre of the image, runs about 80 pixels to the right and ends in the middle of the image. This grid causes another image to be faded in which is used later in the sequence. Corresponding to the luminance values of the individual vertical pixel lines, all images which come between the current frame and the frame which only actually occurs later in the sequence are then faded in.

time displacement

The effect of a displacement grid is determined by the characteristics of the grid or the map used for this grid. The concept of the colour gradation offers many opportunities to make systematic changes to film material or motion graphics. Any motifs and sequences can be used as a model. If motifs are systematically created for use as models, this method in itself can generate sequences which are very interesting and the viewer cannot easily see how they were created. It is always relevant which parameters the brightness values are transferred to.

In these examples, the brightness values of the masks used are transferred to the fading in of frames from the future. The brightness value of the displacement map decides which of the future frames the fade-in image is taken from. In places where the map has a colour gradation and every pixel line therefore has a different brightness value, so it enables a line of another frame to be displayed pixel by pixel. This creates the visualisation of two images which originate at different points in time and the time sequence in only one image.

RULE [A displacement map which changes during the animation. In this way, it determines which frames are faded into the current frame.]

This example [522] shows how the gradation shifts within the luminance mask. As described on the right, its values are linked with the fading in of later frames into the current frame. The relationship between the present and the future, which is visible in each individual picture, changes in a similar way to the vertical shift of the gradation during the sequence.

The effect of displacement maps depends not only on their structural design, but also on their dynamic use. A simple gradation in a luminance mask can be used as an animated layer to give the sequences greater complexity and make them appear more attractive. If the luminance mask is animated, its dynamic character influences the effects that it creates. Structural changes within the mask can also have interesting effects, and when used they look like complex animations.

[520]

[521]

[522]

Displacement map at the beginning, the middle and the end of the animation.

[510.mov/14]

[510.mov/15]

[510.mov/16–21]

[510.mov/4–13] Stills from the animation
[517] Displacement map
[518] Displacement map and real footage
[519] Stills from the animation
[520] Displacement map
[521] Displacement map and real footage
[522] Sequence from the animation
[510.mov/14–21] Stills from the animation

displacing

>SIZE >VOLUME >POSITION TIME

Displacement of time as a proportional visualisation of relationships

GRID: 2D grid, 4D grid
PRINCIPLE: Using changes of real time as a grid
METHOD: Displacing time
EXAMPLE: Clock face and time animation for TV
CONTEXT: 018, 028, 044, 088
MOVIES: 523.mov, 526.mov

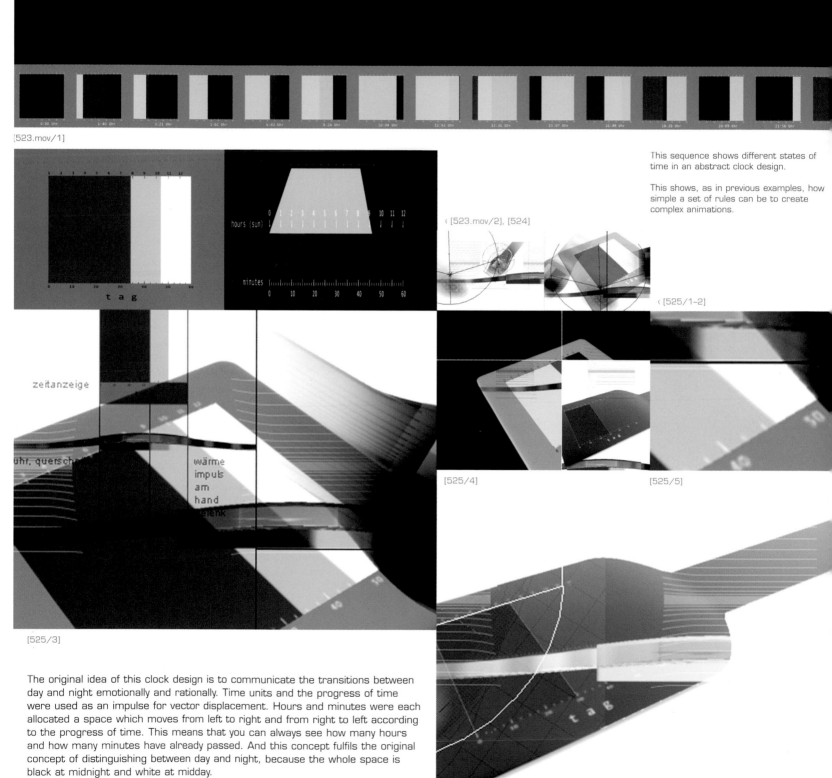

[523.mov/1]

This sequence shows different states of time in an abstract clock design.

This shows, as in previous examples, how simple a set of rules can be to create complex animations.

‹ [523.mov/2], [524]

‹ [525/1-2]

zeitanzeige

uhr, querschn...

wärme
impuls
am
hand
...lenk

[525/4]

[525/5]

[525/3]

The original idea of this clock design is to communicate the transitions between day and night emotionally and rationally. Time units and the progress of time were used as an impulse for vector displacement. Hours and minutes were each allocated a space which moves from left to right and from right to left according to the progress of time. This means that you can always see how many hours and how many minutes have already passed. And this concept fulfils the original concept of distinguishing between day and night, because the whole space is black at midnight and white at midday.

[525/6]

A direct implementation of time in picture form is also used in these animations. They were developed for a television station. The passage of time can be visualised in very different ways by displacement transformations. It all depends on which parameters are manipulated by the values gained from the time analysis.

In this animation seconds are visualised by the movement of the diagonal lines from right to left. Every second, another line becomes visible.

[526.mov/1]

[526.mov/2]

[526.mov/3]

The last 10 seconds before the next programme are visualised by adding the solid yellow dots below the timer. At the same time, the row with the dots moves to the centre of the screen.

[526.mov/4–5]

In this animation the seconds are shown by the rotation of a graphical element. It moves along the face of the clock; indistinct at first, then increasingly clear. In the last 20 seconds the movement along the face of the clock becomes very distinct. The passage of time is displayed proportionally.

[523.mov/1] Sequence from a clock animation
[523.mov/2] Still from the animation
[524] Functional principle of the clock
[525/1–4] Design study
[525/5] Detail
[525/6] Design study
[526.mov/1–5] Stills and sequence from a clock animation for television

deforming
deforming

Design methods which are actually directed more at generating graphical objects themselves than at defining principles to act within a scene are also described as grids for moving pictures. In the spatial changes of objects or viewing distances, rules were also generated which determine the way the objects behave or change, so these rules are also referred to as »grids«. They can always be combined with other rules – for example with a time (4D) grid, with paths or with behaviours. These rules can determine the appearance of an object, the changes to its form, the type and direction of its movement, the timing and the dynamics.

These grids which relate to the design of objects and changes to these objects can also be very powerful and comprehensive, so that they define all rules for the animation. They are used as design aids to induce a striking change of the objects within a defined period. This means that the use of additional grids for timing and movement might be superfluous.

The following grids are based on the principle of changing the three-dimensional form of one or more objects more or less continuously. This can mean, for example, that the movement, the form or the viewing angle are changed by self-defined laws. It becomes evident how great effects can be created with very simple means.

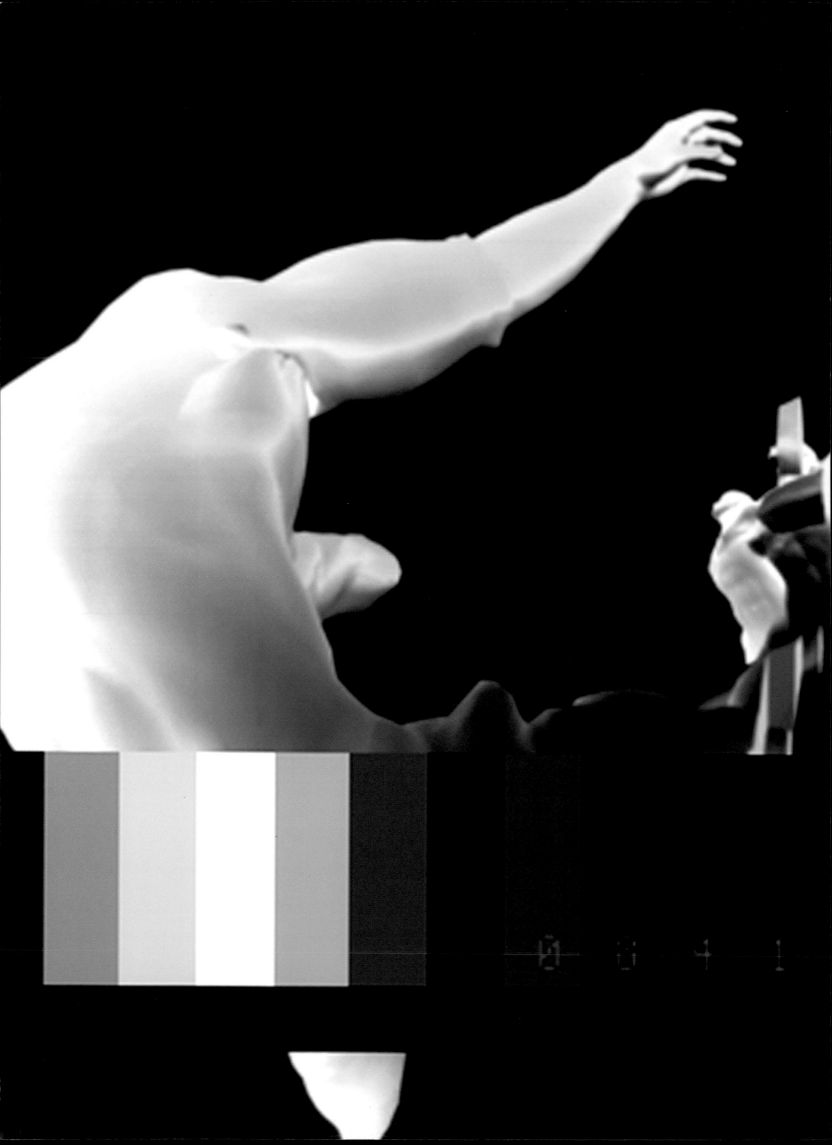

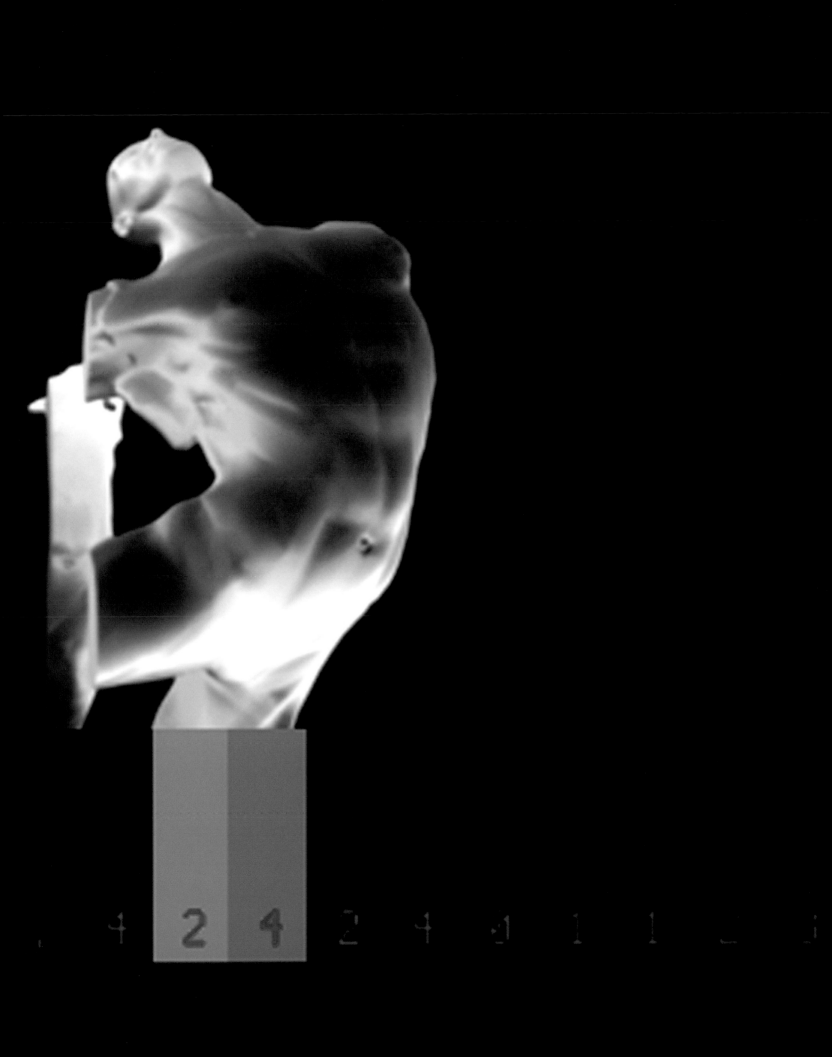

deforming

MERGING >DESTRUCTION >REPETITION >PENETRATION >TORSION >EXPANSION

Merging objects of differing material consistency can create new meanings and new aesthetic effects

GRID: 3D grid
PRINCIPLE: Merging objects of differing material properties
METHOD: Combination of technology and body
EXAMPLE: Extreme sports animation
CONTEXT: 018, 034, 038, 106
MOVIE: 601.mov

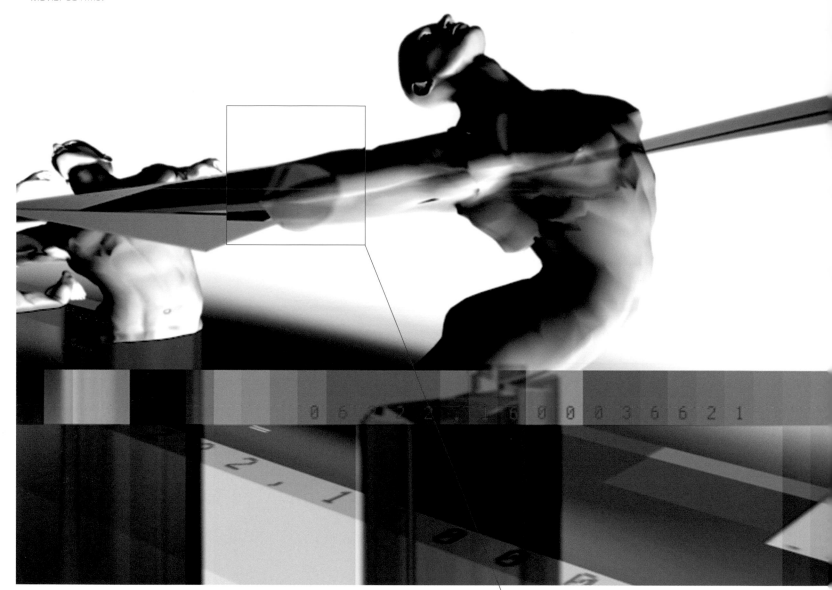

[601.mov/1]

extreme sports

The screenings for the Nea Awards 2001, an international competition for extreme sports, were shown as a live display during the prize award ceremony. For each sport, an animation was created to accompany the nominations. The idea of the design is to show the effect that the strength of the extreme sports participant, who loves to go beyond his or her own limitations, would have if it were not restricted by the boundaries of the human body. This gave rise to a series of sequences which present abstract bodies »frozen« in time to illustrate the respective sports. The visible exaggeration and brutality give expression to the unlimited force which would act on the body if there were no physical boundaries to prevent this.

All sequences follow global rules – such as colouring, timing and the type of design – but the appearance of the sequences is largely determined by the striking visual character of the deformation of the body. The rules that were followed are described in the following pages.

INFO [The process of sailing and the bodies merge to form a sculpture which, in its design and movement, associatively conveys this simultaneity of the object and the process.]

merging

This sequence represents the category of sailing. It shows a figure which has itself partly been transformed into a sail. Apart from the bodily deformation, the main feature of this animation – like the other sequences at the Nea Awards 2001 – is the use of slow-continuous movements of the bodies which are »frozen« in the dynamics of their action. This makes the animation appear very monumental. The process of sailing and the bodies merge to form a sculpture which, in its design and movement, associatively conveys this simultaneity of the object and the process.

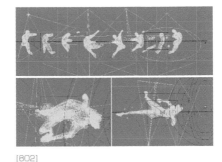

[802]

‹ [601.mov/2–3]

~[601.mov/4]

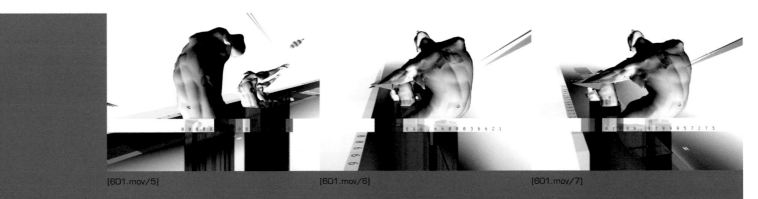

[601.mov/5]　　　　[601.mov/6]　　　　[601.mov/7]

[601.mov/1] Still from the animation
[802] Construction of a scene in 3D
[601.mov/2–3] Stills from the animation
[601.mov/4] Extract from the sequence
[601.mov/5–7] Stills from the animation

deforming

>MERGING **DESTRUCTION** >REPETITION >PENETRATION >TORSION >EXPANSION

Virtual processes, like power or force, in a time-slicing representation determine the character of this animation

GRID: 3D grid
PRINCIPLE: Using destruction as grid
METHOD: Creating virtual explosions
EXAMPLE: Extreme sports animation
CONTEXT: 018, 034, 038, 106
MOVIES: 601.mov, 604.mov

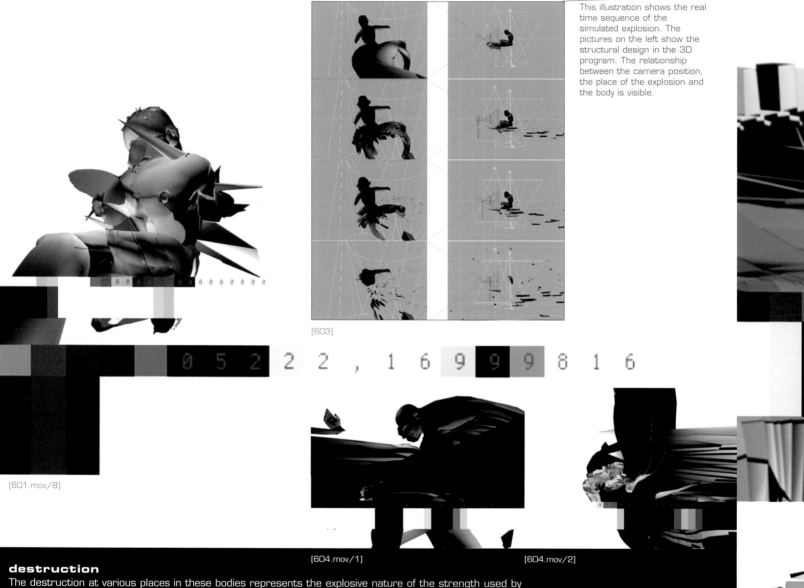

This illustration shows the real time sequence of the simulated explosion. The pictures on the left show the structural design in the 3D program. The relationship between the camera position, the place of the explosion and the body is visible.

[603]

[601.mov/8]

[604.mov/1]

[604.mov/2]

destruction

The destruction at various places in these bodies represents the explosive nature of the strength used by extreme sports participants in their sports. They are virtual scenarios which visualise the strength which the sports participants would exercise, and the strain they would bear, if they could go beyond the limits of their own bodies.

The idea behind the design was to place explosions at various points in the body, and subsequently to animate them at the moment of explosion as three-dimensional objects using the »time-slicing« method. No other grid was added to this effect with its very extreme appearance. The bodies rotate slowly and continuously around their own axis, giving them a monumental appearance.

0 5 2 2 2 , 1 6 9 9 9 9 8 1 6 8 9

[601.mov/9]

[601.mov/10]

The area of the virtual explosion in a still.

[603] Structure of a scene in 3D
[601.mov/8] Still from the animation
[604.mov/1-2] Stills from the animation
[601.mov/9] Still from the animation
[601.mov/10] Sequence from the animation

deforming

>MERGING >DESTRUCTION REPETITION >PENETRATION >TORSION >EXPANSION

The grids in these sequences were created by the use of spatial and temporal tracks

GRID: 3D grid, 4D grid
PRINCIPLE: Using repetition as grid
METHOD: Creating spatial and temporal tracks
EXAMPLE: Extreme sports animation
CONTEXT: 018, 028, 038, 106
MOVIE: 604.mov

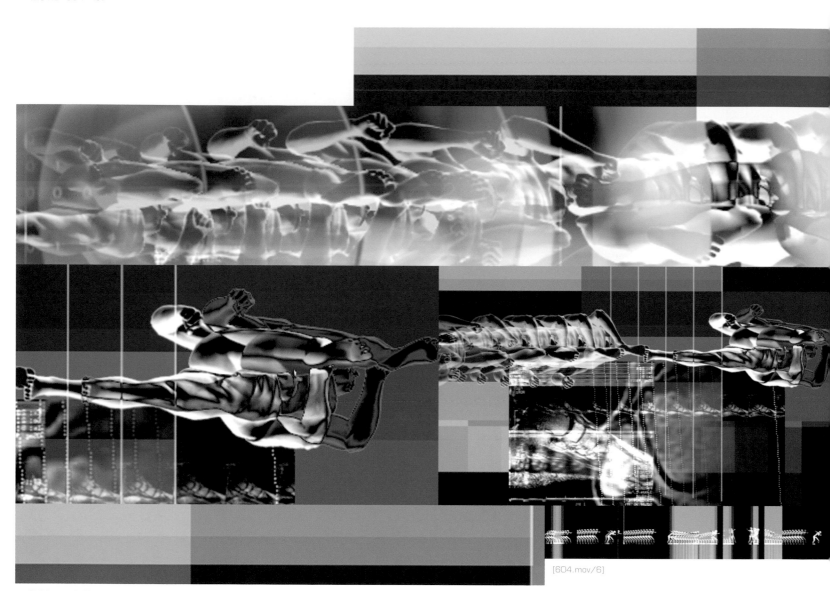

[604.mov/6]

[604.mov/3–5]

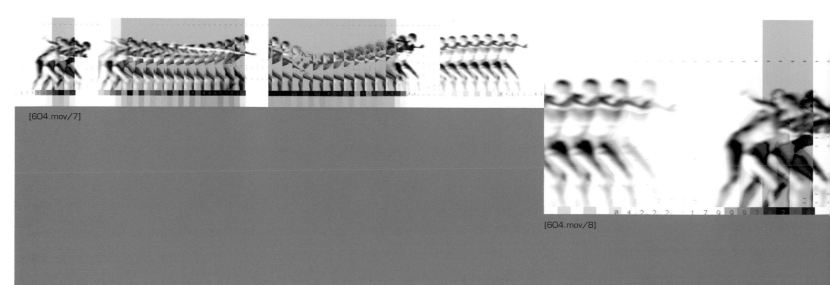

[604.mov/7]

[604.mov/8]

INFO [The pictures in this sequence have been shifted in space and time. Even with this very simple technique of creating tracks it is quickly possible to come up with an interesting animation.]

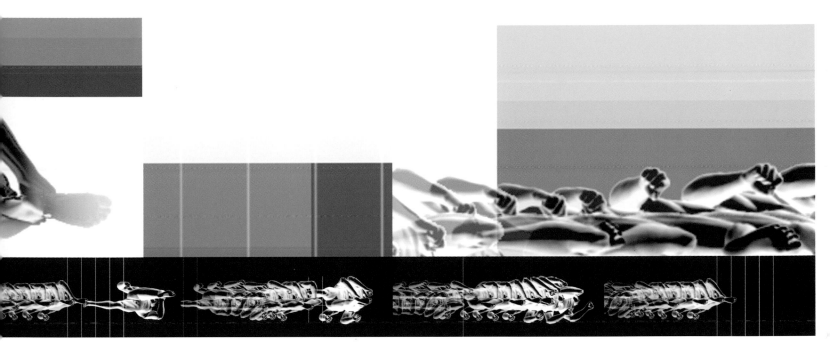

[604.mov/9], [604.mov/10]

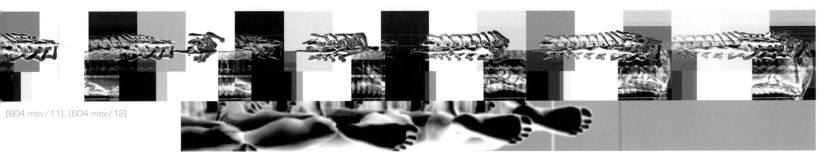

[604.mov/11], [604.mov/12]

[604.mov/13]

repetition

These sequences were given their grid by a relatively simple and well-known principle, the use of spatial and temporal tracks. In this process, one set of rules was used for the time and one set of rules for the treatment of space. The representation of past phases of the animation in the respective current image creates some completely new visual units, that are perceived as bodies. Their form is generated by vertically shifting the respective previous images to the left. This composition, which the viewer perceives as a new, virtual body, moves in a very strange and yet fascinating manner (cf. the video material). By contrast with the previous examples, the dynamics can be seen as such here, too.

[604.mov/3–5] Stills and sequence from the animation: runner
[604.mov/6–8] Stills and sequence from the animation: surfer
[604.mov/9–13] Stills and sequence from the animation: runner

deforming

The rotation of a 3D object and the change of the viewing distance which is caused by the different spatial expansions of the object create the grid in this sequence

GRID: 3D grid
PRINCIPLE: Using penetration as grid
METHOD: Observing penetrated object
EXAMPLE: Motion graphic footage
CONTEXT: 018, 034, 106, 133
MOVIE: 605.mov

[605.mov/1–3]

[605.mov/4]

[605.mov/5]

penetration

The set of this sequence is very simple, but it should still be mentioned. A Boolean operation has been added to a twisted object. The object merely rotates around its centre. A camera which is in a fixed position films the scene. As the camera is relatively close to the centre in the cut-out section, the images partly show the interior of the object, and partly its exterior. The attractive interchange between exterior and interior views of the object seems to create a special timing. However, this animation does not contain a 4D grid, and there is no change in its speed. This effect results naturally from the changes in the viewing distance. The form and rotation of the object and the mode of viewing are sufficient to create the visual situations.

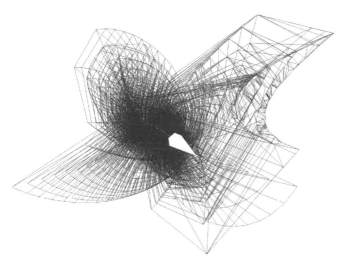

[606]

[605.mov/6-11]

No extra grid has been added to this animation, no manipulation of the speed and no spatial change during the animation. The aesthetic charm of this animation results solely from the structure and design of the object and the fact that the interior of the object is viewed for part of the time, creating interesting images because of its intricate structure.

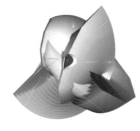

[607/1]

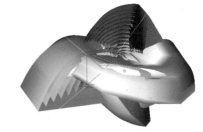

[607/2]

3D object that rotates around its centre.

[605.mov/1-3] Stills and sequence from the animation
[605.mov/4-5] Stills from the object animation
[606] 3D structure of the object
[605.mov/6-11] Stills and sequence from the animation
[607/1] View and camera position of the 3D model
[607/2] View and camera position of the 3D model

deforming

>MERGING >DESTRUCTION >REPETITION >PENETRATION TORSION >EXPANSION

Two combined 3D objects and the addition of a deformation object determine the essence of this animation

GRID: 3D grid
PRINCIPLE: Using torsion as grid
METHOD: Creating deformation by twisting objects
EXAMPLE: Motion graphic footage
CONTEXT: 018, 034, 038, 106
MOVIE: –

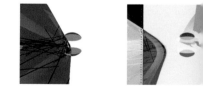

[608/1]

[608/2]

[608/3]

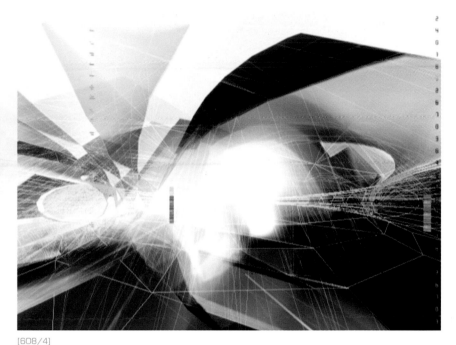

[608/4]

Basic structure of the 3D object.

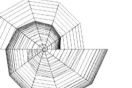

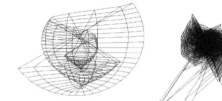

[609/1] [609/2] [609/3]

[608/5]

torsion

This animation is largely determined by the structure of a 3D object. Two spirals were placed opposite each other. A deformation object placed in the centre causes this structure to twist within itself in the centre. The 3D object rotates through 360 degrees around its centre. A camera placed very close to the centre provides the images.

Some of the graphical elements were added during post-production, such as the two semi-spheres in the centre, the lines and the coloured surfaces. This example shows how easily an interesting animation can be created by defining a few simple rules. Apart from the grid that determines the 3D object, no other changes have been made to the dimensions of space and time during the animation.

[608/1] Still from the animation
[608/2] Sequence from the animation
[608/3-4] Stills from the animation
[609/1] 3D structure, top view
[609/2] 3D structure, side view
[609/3] 3D structure, camera view
[608/5] Sequence from the animation

deforming

>MERGING >DESTRUCTION >REPETITION >PENETRATION >TORSION EXPANSION

The structure and the spatial change of a 3D object over time determine the grid of this sequence

GRID: 3D grid
PRINCIPLE: Using expansion as grid
METHOD: Creating spatial change of a 3D object
EXAMPLE: Motion graphic footage
CONTEXT: 018, 034, 038, 106
MOVIE: 610.mov

[610.mov/1]

[610.mov/2]

[610.mov/3]

[610.mov/4]

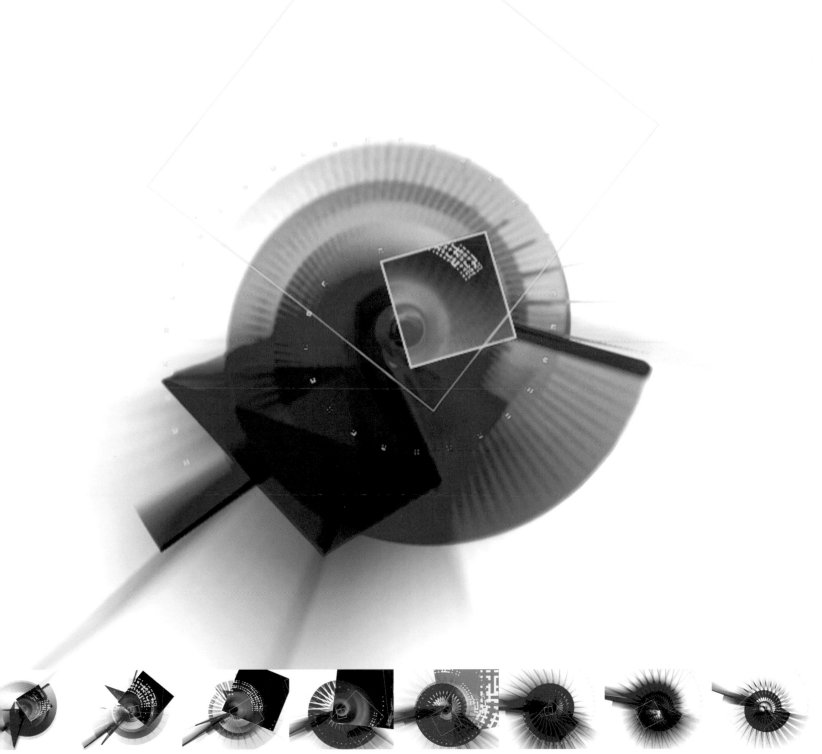

[610.mov/5], [610.mov/6]

expansion

The structure, change and behaviour of a 3D object over time determine the grid of this sequence. By contrast with the previous examples, the object changes in its spatial structure during the animation. Apart from a rotation around its own centre, a deformation is used here which changes the object over time in its vertical and horizontal expansion. This deformation was not caused by deformation objects, but by the definition of expansion and growth.

The visual parameters were added during post-production, such as colours and the square, which also rotates in accordance with the rotation of the object, and which becomes bigger at the same time. The structure of the illustration is determined in the last resort by the 3D object and its defined changes, and this generates an interesting animation.

This procedure shows how easily, with simple principles, new forms of design can be created quickly.

[610.mov/1–2] 3D structure
[610.mov/3] Still from the animation
[610.mov/4] Sequence from the 3D structure
[610.mov/5] Still from the animation
[610.mov/6] Sequence from the animation

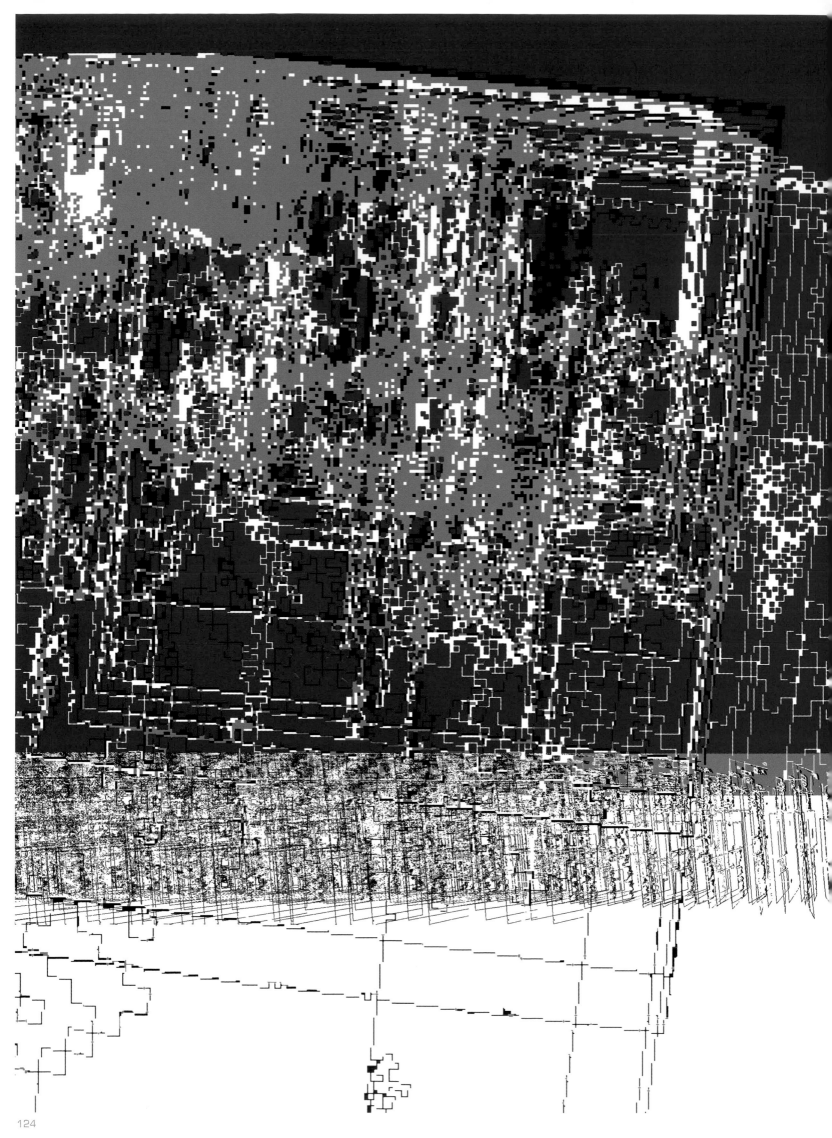

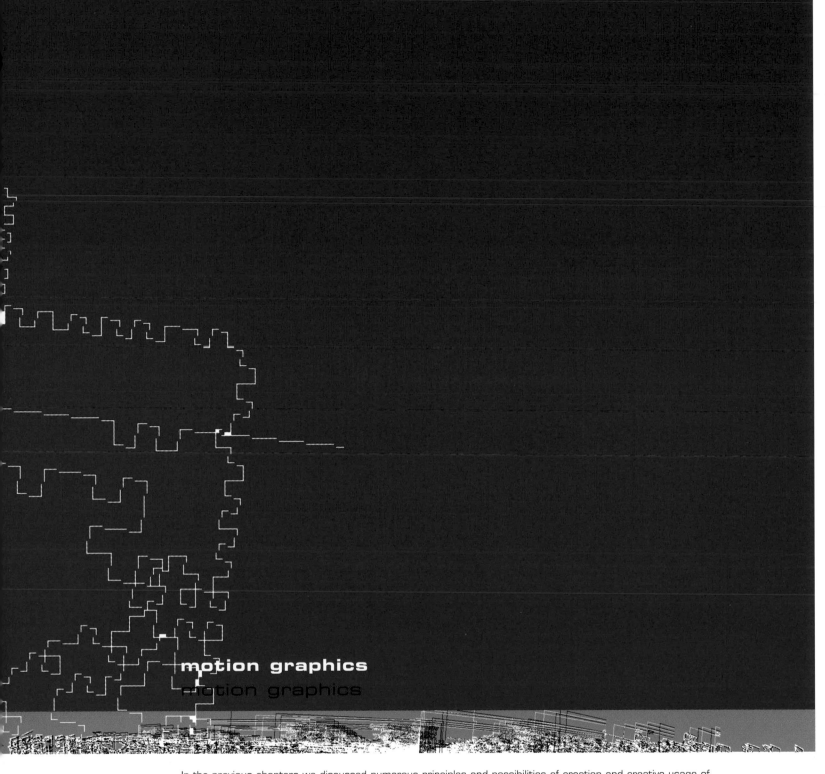

motion graphics
motion graphics

In the previous chapters we discussed numerous principles and possibilities of creation and creative usage of grids. External circumstances or technical realities can additionally influence the basic behaviour and look of an animation. The movement of a person or the architecture of a building can for instance become the structural model for an animation. Digital and analogue elements are seamlessly merged and the change of position of a person or the structure of a room becomes a grid. With extreme specifications like animations that only last for one second, time can also be regarded as a grid.

Most animations use numerous »grids« and rarely work with only one kind. Nevertheless there is always one grid or aspect that has an overall impact on the dramaturgy of a sequence and is therefore dominant. Even when using grids as the main support in the creation of dramaturgy, it is unavoidable to manipulate individual details or complete animations by setting key frames manually. Hence the room for creativity is endless, but equally the effort to create dramaturgy or movement increases considerably. The creation of motion graphics for brands often requires not only the usage of grids, but also exact manual generation of dynamics and dramaturgy.

motion graphics

SPATIAL ANIMATION >CHARACTER ANIMATION >TYPOGRAPHY ANIMATION >LOGO ANIMATION

The grid is based on a sequential principle. The design reacts flexibly to the mood of the visitors

GRID: 3D grid, 4D grid
PRINCIPLE: Using sequential arrangement as a grid
METHOD: Creating repetition of object movement
EXAMPLE: Environmental design for a media festival
CONTEXT: 032, 038, 085, 124
MOVIE: –

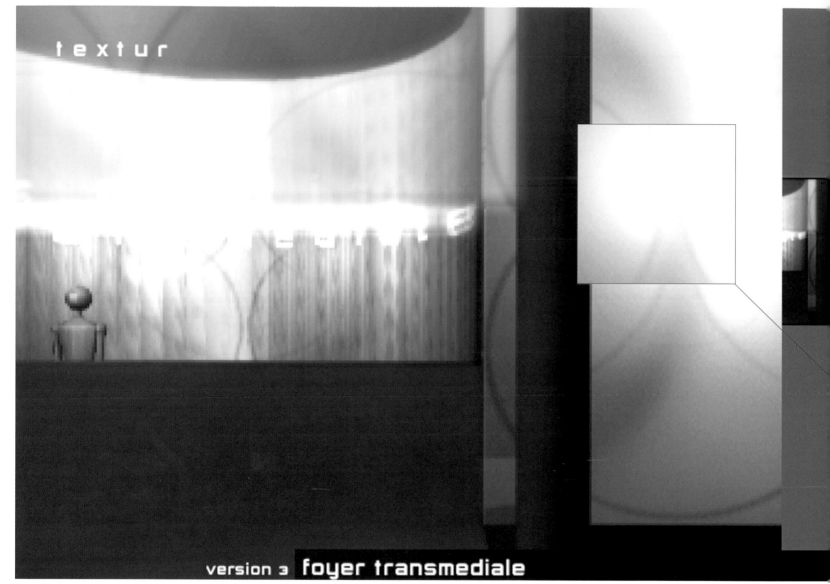

[701/1]

transmediale

The design of this environment is based on a sequential grid. The design for digital wallpaper was created for the media in the room design of the Berlin media festival »Transmediale«. The underlying idea was to create an irritation in the perception of the beholder. Projected patterns on the walls were to change minimally at a very slow speed. Almost imperceptibly, so that the viewers do not know whether the image is moving at all. Sometimes the foreground and background moved in relation to each other, sometimes unsharp light effects moved across the animation.

Due to the principle of the sequential arrangement, only one video sequence needed to be developed for each environment. The design of the animations was created so that they could be smoothly placed in sequence. This was achieved by the even disappearance and reappearance of elements. Like in the design of fabric samples, for example, each cut-off at the edge of a screen is generated by the cut-off of the same motif on the opposite edge of the screen.

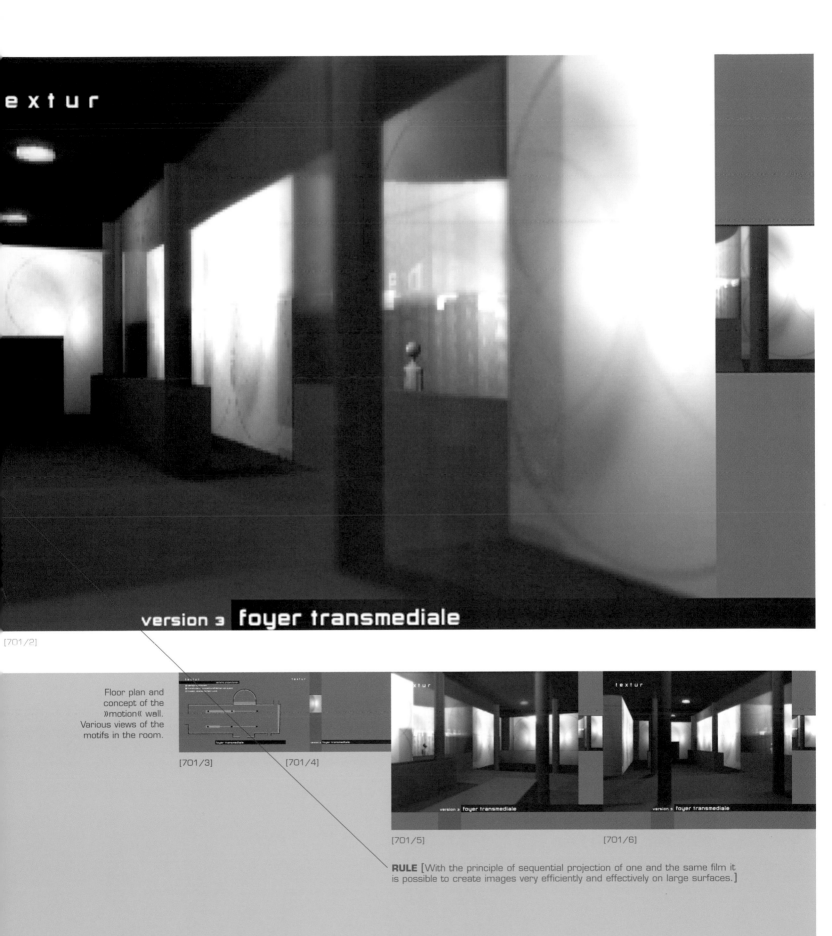

version 3 **foyer transmediale**

[701/2]

Floor plan and
concept of the
»motion« wall.
Various views of the
motifs in the room.

[701/3]   [701/4]

[701/5]   [701/6]

RULE [With the principle of sequential projection of one and the same film it
is possible to create images very efficiently and effectively on large surfaces.]

[701/1–6] View of the foyer, design 3

motion graphics

SPATIAL ANIMATION >CHARACTER ANIMATION >TYPOGRAPHY ANIMATION >LOGO ANIMATION

The floor plan of the room determines the grid of this animation

GRID: 3D grid, 4D grid
PRINCIPLE: Using real architecture as grid
METHOD: Creating visual irritation, creating visual interaction
EXAMPLE: Environmental design for a media festival and for an event
CONTEXT: 032, 038, 084, 124
MOVIE: –

[702/1] ~ [703/1] ~

[703/2] [703/3] [703/4]

[702/2] [702/3]

[704/1] [704/2]

Various colour and pattern designs make it possible to create completely different moods for the room in a short time. This was necessary because the festival was held both during the daytime and in the evening, and because the visitors were in different »moods« at different times. The programme in the evening was dominated by the surroundings, whereas simple colours and shapes were featured during the daytime.

[705]

[706/1] [706/2] [706/3] [706/4]

[707]

abb

This study for an unspecified company is based on the floor plan of the room in which the event was to take place. The room consisted of a corridor which made up a rectangle. It was therefore possible to situate the projectors in the centre of the building but outside the corridors. This meant that the viewers inside the corridors would be forced to interact with the projections. They could control the events interactively by their actions. When the visitor touched the beam of light of the laser spotlights that shone down to the ground in front of each motif, further sequences were triggered. The projection of the images is therefore dependent on the position of the viewer who triggers the sequence of pictures when he or she reaches a specific point – in passing, so to speak.

The floor plan of the installation room inspired the narrative grid and the projection arrangement.

[708]

motion graphics

SPATIAL ANIMATION >CHARACTER ANIMATION >TYPOGRAPHY ANIMATION >LOGO ANIMATION

Order by spatial and temporal parameters of the environment and the visitors

GRID: 3D grid, 4D grid
PRINCIPLE: Using architecture and visitors' movement as grid
METHOD: Triggering by the visitors' movement
EXAMPLE: Environmental design study
CONTEXT: 032, 038, 050, 084, 124
MOVIE: –

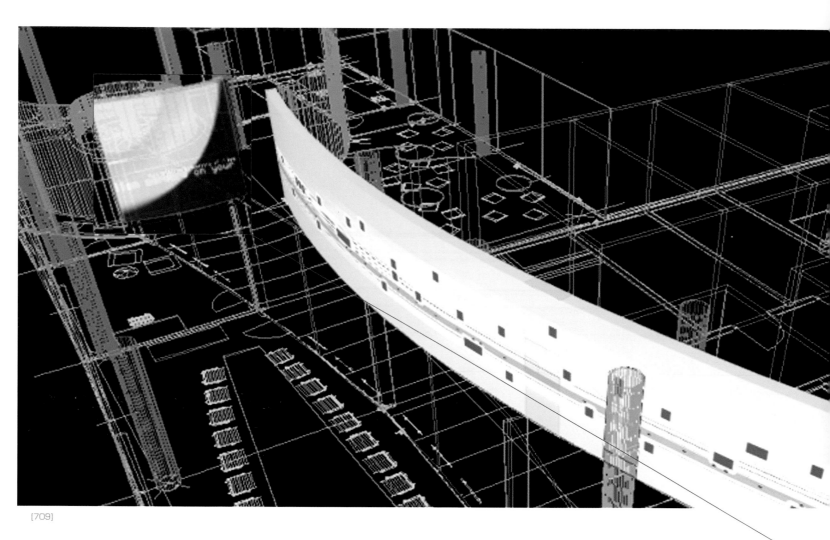

[709]

lucent

This concept for a media environment is based on the idea of including the visitors to the room in the sequences, and at the same time integrating the technical installations into the environment. Monitors were set into a designed wall. Sensors were used to harness the movement of the visitors as an impulse to control individual sequences. This triggered both individual animations and sequence changes in the animations which were in progress. The content of the animations was mainly a playful elementary treatment of the visual design components of the company logo.

[710/1]

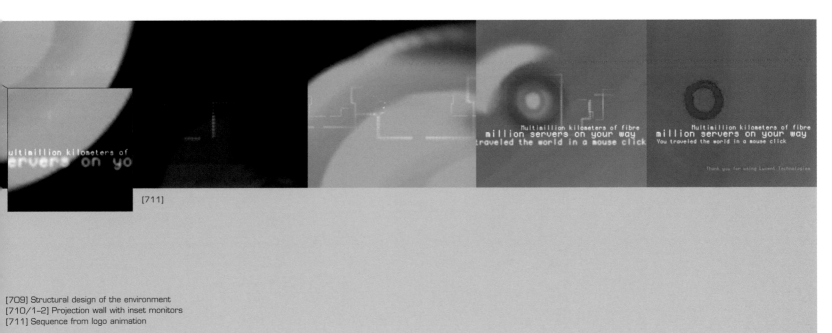

[710/2]

[711]

[709] Structural design of the environment
[710/1-2] Projection wall with inset monitors
[711] Sequence from logo animation

motion graphics

SPATIAL ANIMATION >CHARACTER ANIMATION >TYPOGRAPHY ANIMATION >LOGO ANIMATION

Physical behaviours and sequential orders determine the impact of this large screen animation
Behaviour and the micro and macro view of objects and scenarios give this design its character

GRID: 3D grid, 4D grid
PRINCIPLE: Using behaviour and interrelations of physical models as grid
METHOD: Creating vibration patterns, sequential arrangement and micro/macro views
EXAMPLE: Environmental design at an international car fair and for an energy corporation company event
CONTEXT: 042, 054, 066, 084, 124
MOVIE: –

RULE [The principle of the sequential arrangement of motifs can be very effective when the
appropriate 4D grid is used.]

[712/1]

[712/2]

[712/3]

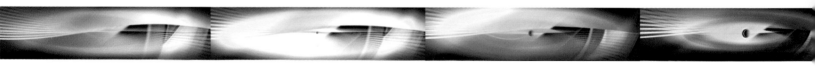

[712/4-7]

opel

This animation was used as a large-scale projection on an LED wall measuring 17 x 4 metres at an
international motor show. The aim was not to visualise the functional advantages of the cars presented,
but the beauty of form which could be found in numerous details of the new line of cars manufactured by
Opel. It was especially important to communicate the aesthetics and dynamics of the new models.
Inspired by the forms of the new cars, the presentation mainly used digitally generated vibration patterns
and sequential arrangements. The size of the projection surface gave the abstract animations of the
vibration graphics an extremely attractive force. The attention of the viewer was further enhanced by the
fading-in and animation of individual details. The sequential arrangement of film showing a car moving
towards the viewer also had great appeal. The viewer was very much emotionally involved in the
animation as a result of the projection size, the design methods and the dynamics of the sequence.

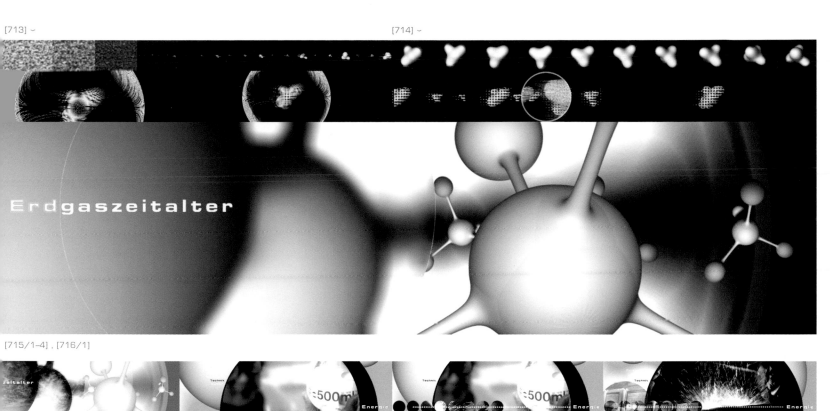

Erdgaszeitalter

[715/1–4] , [716/1]

[716/2–5]

[716/6]

[716/7]

INFO [Dynamic 3D models inspired by the formation of molecules offered numerous opportunities to project other visuals in these sequences. The 3D models were used as micro views, macro views, interior and exterior views and in spatial formations.]

ruhrgas

The behaviour of molecules and the possibility to view the motifs in a micro and macro view is the basic idea behind this large-screen animation. The company history of an energy corporation was presented on a projection surface of 30 x 10 metres. The gas molecules were the dominant element in the sequence.

[712/1–7] Sequences and stills of a large scale projection for Opel
[713] Sequence of micro/macro views of a molecule model
[714] Sequence of a 3D molecule model used to display images
[715/1–4] Stills of a micro/macro view animation of a molecule model used as grid
[716/1–7] Stills from a large-scale projection for the »Ruhrgas« company

motion graphics

SPATIAL ANIMATION >CHARACTER ANIMATION >TYPOGRAPHY ANIMATION >LOGO ANIMATION

This media environment for a theatre production is based on motion tracking, the use of
a gravitation behaviour and random-based algorithm, which generate controlled order in space

GRID: 3D grid, 4D grid
PRINCIPLE: Using movement of actors/media and behaviours as grid
METHOD: Motion tracking, gravitation and random algorithm
EXAMPLE: Media staging »looking for mies«
CONTEXT: 032, 050, 058, 074, 086
MOVIE: –

[717/1]

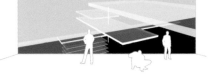

[717/2]

[717/3]

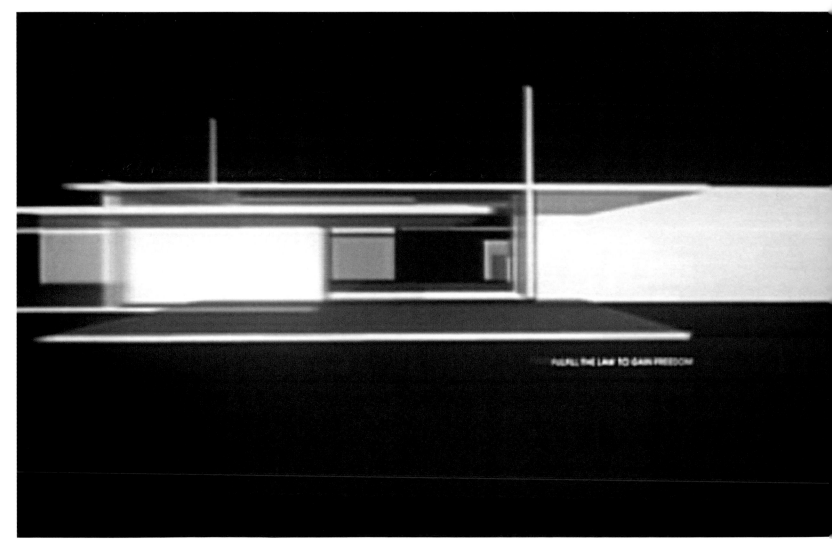

[718]

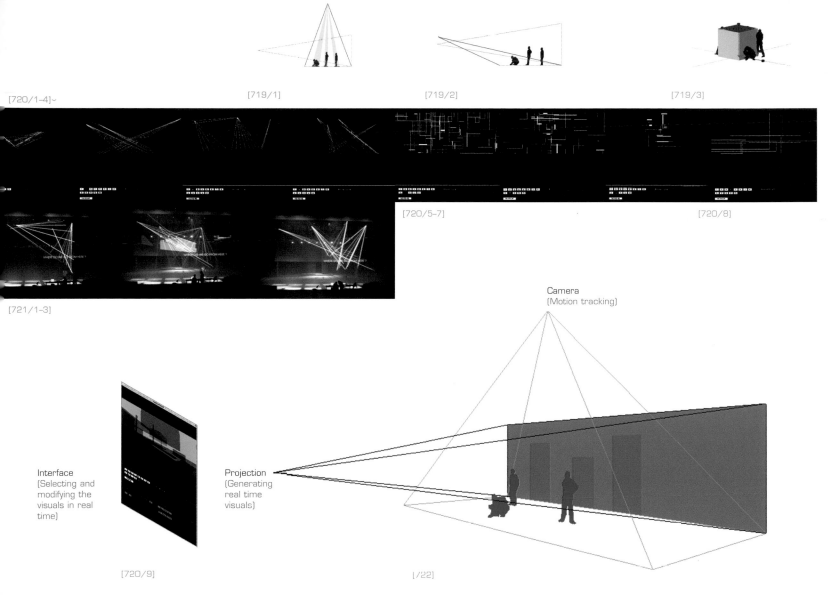

[720/1–4]~

[719/1]

[719/2]

[719/3]

[720/5–7]

[720/8]

[721/1–3]

Camera
(Motion tracking)

Interface
(Selecting and
modifying the
visuals in real
time)

Projection
(Generating
real time
visuals)

[720/9]

[722]

looking for mies

This example shows a media production for a piece on Ludwig Mies van der Rohe. Various different methods to create moving image sequences were used. Essentially all visuals are based on motion tracking, gravitation and random algorithms. One idea was to steer visuals by using changes on stage. Another idea brought to bear was the usage of a 3D-engine to create in real time, following the typical proportion of Mies van der Rohe's buildings, a virtual pavilion which one could navigate through. The third idea is a randomly driven generation of a floor plan, which in real time slowly expands to fill the whole picture, again following typical proportionalities used by Mies van der Rohe.

A projection encompassing the whole stage was driven by human or object movement on stage. Every change on stage was registered and the gained data could then be transformed into various visual representations in real time. Via an interface, 8 different types of visuals could be selected. These included bright vertical or horizontal stripes, perspectively represented cuboids, laser beams that followed a person or move in the respective place.

A video camera recorded all changes on stage and transferred the data to a computer, which analysed the x and y coordinates of the moving objects. These would then be used as impulse to drive the behaviour of the visualisation. The acquired values were applied to the graphic elements on screen, as well as luminance and speed.

[717/1–3] Concept sketch, using the stage and performers as a projection room
[718] Still of a sequence generating architecture through behaviours and algorithm
[719/1–3] Sets of the motion tracking construction with camera and projection
[720/1–9] Screenshots of the interface with different motifs displayed
[721/1–3] Photos taken during the rehearsal of the performance
[722] Construction of the motion tracking stage set with camera and projection

motion graphics

>SPATIAL ANIMATION CHARACTER ANIMATION >TYPOGRAPHY ANIMATION >LOGO ANIMATION

Motion capturings, addition and appending of motion sequences are the basis of creating complex character animations

GRID: 3D grid, 4D grid
PRINCIPLE: Using movement paths as grid for character animation
METHOD: Capturing of motion, addition and appending of action sequences
EXAMPLE: Character animation of robots
CONTEXT: 029, 050, 058, 145
MOVIE: –

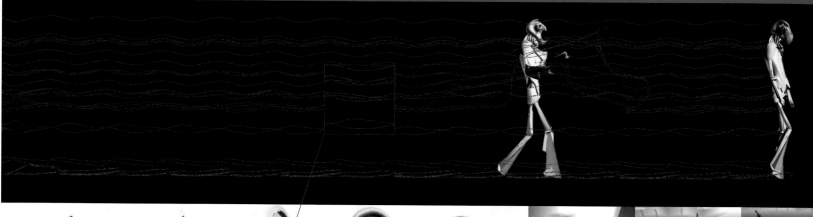

[723], [724/1–8]

body in motion

The traces of a movement can be visualised by long exposure, which creates a shape that represents the path of a movement. Reversed, this principle can be applied to use a graphic as a pattern, a grid for the animation of a movement. Objects will then travel along its lines.

In the field of character animation, motion paths are often used as grids to automatically generate complex motion sequences (e.g. walking, running, fighting etc.). As shown in the illustration above, these movements can be enhanced additionally. During »walking« for instance, a figure can also be given an »arm movement« without interrupting the flow of »walking«.

[725]

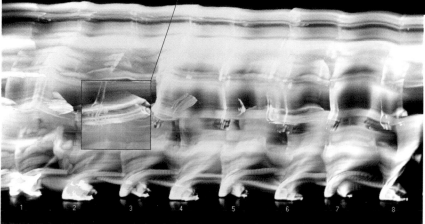

[726] Long exposure of a walking figure. The movement is visible as »shape«.

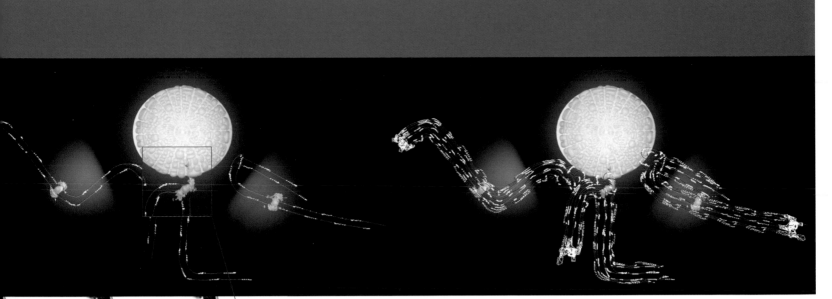

[728/1–3]

[727/1-2]

This illustration shows, in an overhead view, a plasma egg reactor and the motion paths of the robots. Three robots walk to the »reactor«, collect plasma eggs, turn around and leave again. The sequence of »walking« was combined with the sequence of »picking« and »turning«. Complex animations are often created in an additive process by stringing together partial sequences.

[728/4–8]

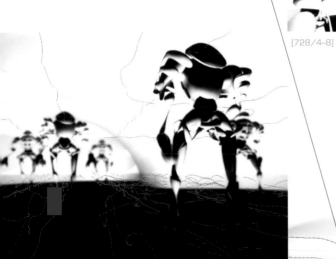

[729]

body in action

Animations that describe complex motion sequences are divided into single sequences that show simple, partial movements. Optionally, the individual sequences can be strung together. In this way, the »walk« of a robot is followed by the »collection« of a plasma egg etc. The scenes are linked together and only in the sum represent a concise and complex sequence.

[730] ›

[728/9–13]

[723] Visualisation of the movement paths of a robot walking
[724/1–8] Sequence of a robot moving its head
[725] Visualisation of the movement paths and footsteps of robots
[726] Picture of a person walking taken with a long exposure
[727/1–2] Overhead view of the robots' movement paths
[728/1–13] Stills from a sequence where robots collect eggs
[729] Visualisation of the movement path of robots walking
[730] Visualisation of the movement path of the robots in action

motion graphics

Relating objects by inverse cinematics and the use of motion capturings is the essence of robot animation
The definition of interaction behaviour serves to create the attitude of the interacting robots

GRID: 4D grid
PRINCIPLE: Using object combination to create smooth motion and movement paths and behaviour as grid
METHOD: Inverse cinematics, motion capturing and interaction behaviour
EXAMPLE: Character animation of one or more robots in action and interacting
CONTEXT: 050, 072, 074, 084
MOVIE: 731.mov

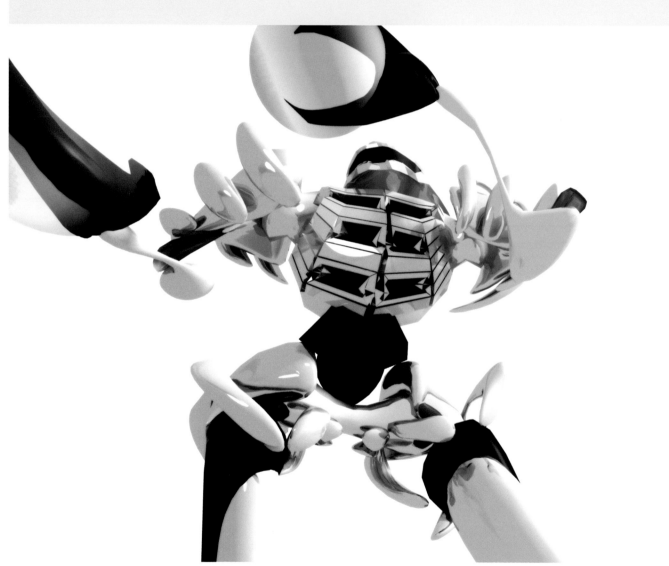

[731.mov/1]

[731.mov/2-9]

body in action

To create the movement of various objects, e.g. a robot's hand or an egg being carried, objects can be linked
together by inverse kinematics. Therefore, either the egg or the robot's hand can be animated, as the linked
object is automatically animated as well. In this way elegant movements can be created without having to
animate each object individually. Originally this technique was developed to animate limbs that are linked
together.

[732/1-6]

[732/7]

[732/8]

[732/9]

[732/10], [732/11-14]

zone of attraction

actor — zone of rejection

neutral zone

position of attraction · neutral position · position of rejection

[733]

body interaction

This animation shows two interacting creatures. A very simple, manually rendered behaviour is applied. It is based on attraction and repulsion. Each body is surrounded by three reactive zones [733]. These determine, depending on the distance between the bodies, the according behaviour, e.g. attraction if both meet in the outer circle and repulsion if both touch in the inner circle. As a basic principle both bodies attract each other until they eventually repulse each other. This happens if a certain state of vicinity is reached and both have entered the repulsion zone.

INFO [The creation and adjustment of interactive behaviour demands utmost precision, as there is only a fine line between controlled and uncontrolled chaos.]

[731.mov/1-9] Stills from a sequence in which a robot is holding an egg
[732/1-14] Stills from a sequence where two robots interact with each other
[733] Grid of the sequence based on the definition of different behaviour zones

motion graphics

>SPATIAL ANIMATION **CHARACTER ANIMATION** >TYPOGRAPHY ANIMATION >LOGO ANIMATION

Mass behaviour based on intelligent particle systems or self-defined rules creates the effect that many objects react automatically to defined impulse events

GRID: 4D grid
PRINCIPLE: Using mass behaviour and self-defined rules as grid
METHOD: Creating intelligent particle systems to animate creatures
EXAMPLE: Swarm animation of small robotic creatures
CONTEXT: 050, 072, 086, 141
MOVIE: –

[734/1–2]

‹ [735/1]

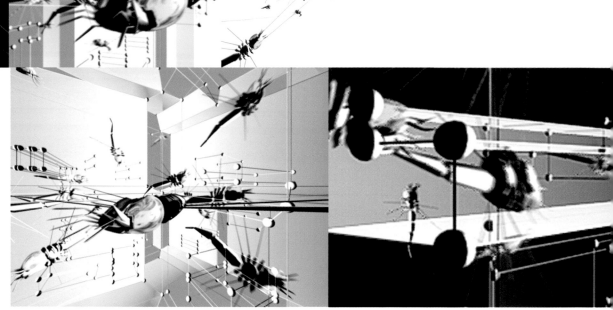

[734/3]   [734/4]

[735/2–9]

intelligent swarm animation

This animation uses intelligent systems of particles. Depending on defined events, for instance the collision of two robots, reactions are determined that relate to a number of objects. A collision can for instance trigger the generation of a new bulk of robots then and there.

[734/5]

intelligent action

Intelligent behaviour can also generate complex sequences of behaviour. Here, the robots only begin to collect »plasma eggs« if their energy level drops, i.e. if they haven't received nourishment for a long time. An interdependence between time and behaviour has been determined that triggers this animation.

[736/1]

[736/2-9]

[734/1-5] Stills from an animated swarm sequence
[735/1-9] Stills of the robot's motion path (grid)
[736/1-9] Stills from a sequence where robots act in a group based on behaviour

The behaviour of a group of creatures is related to one creature. The group is determined by the action of one

GRID: 4D grid
PRINCIPLE: Using behaviour as grid
METHOD: Defining mass behaviour by relating many objects to one
EXAMPLE: Animation of a group of creatures
CONTEXT: 016, 050, 072, 140
MOVIE: –

[737/1–5]

TIP [A slight delay or inaccuracy in the combination of the leading and following object makes the animation seem very lifelike.]

[737/6–8]

[737/9–11]

group of creatures

This animation shows the application of intelligent behaviour on a mass of objects. Depending on certain events, like for instance the turning or moving of the lead creature (in this case the creature with the shell-like covering) it automatically triggers a reaction in the other creatures. All the other creatures follow the actions of the lead figure, no matter when and where the two groups meet. Fluctuations in the reaction of the group are caused by delayed reactions to the impulse or differing speeds of movement. In this way the scene appears very lifelike.

[737/12]

[737/13-20]

[737/1-20] Stills from an animated sequence showing one robotic creature influencing the others

motion graphics

>SPATIAL ANIMATION **CHARACTER ANIMATION** >TYPOGRAPHY ANIMATION >LOGO ANIMATION

Using behaviour based on gravitation and inactivity to create motion in related objects

GRID: 3D grid, 4D grid
PRINCIPLE: Using physical behaviour as grid
METHOD: Defining gravitation and inactivity
EXAMPLE: Artificial life
CONTEXT: 050, 072, 078, 084
MOVIE: 738.mov

[738.mov/1]

>SPATIAL ANIMATION **CHARACTER ANIMATION** >TYPOGRAPHY ANIMATION >LOGO ANIMATION

Using behaviour based on gravitation and inactivity to create motion in related objects

GRID: 3D grid, 4D grid
PRINCIPLE: Using physical behaviour as grid
METHOD: Defining gravitation and inactivity
EXAMPLE: Artificial life
CONTEXT: 050, 072, 078, 084
MOVIE: 738.mov

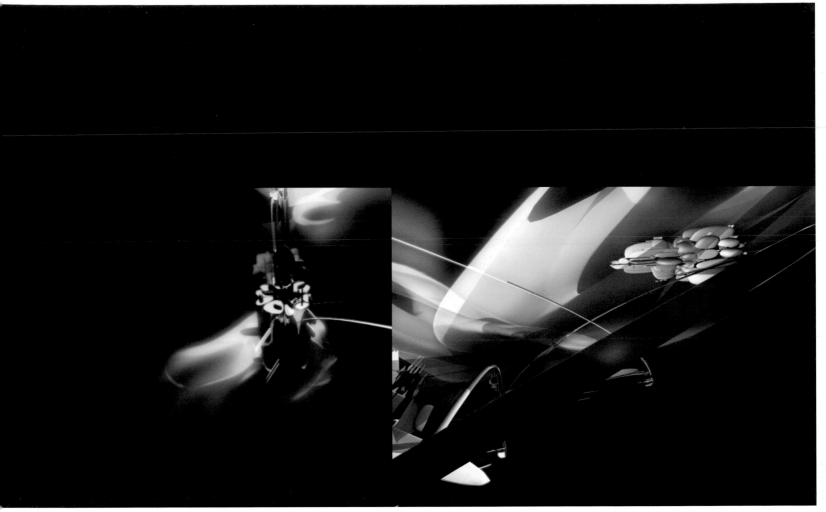

[738.mov/2]   [738.mov/3]

artificial life

This animation uses a behaviour that is based on gravitation and creates an automatic animation by adjusting the parameters. The bright green, amorphic object is linked to the dark green, technoid object in the centre. The movement of the bright green object develops in relation to the object in the centre. It reacts with a slight delay to the movement of the solid body. It has been allocated inertia which results in a natural movement of the bright green object, similar to a piece of cloth in the wind. The material properties of the object as well as its surroundings also have an influence on the appearance of the movement.

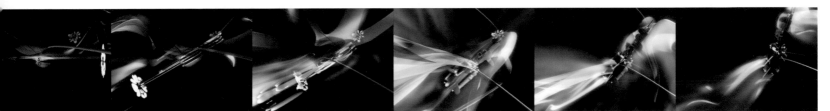

[738.mov/4–9]

[738.mov/1–9] Stills from an artifical life animated sequence

motion graphics

Guiding the viewer's attention and ensuring legibility are the defining factors in these sequences

GRID: 4D grid
PRINCIPLE: Using the guidance of the viewer's attention as grid
METHOD: Creating selected coordinates to display typography
EXAMPLE: Advertising TV clips
CONTEXT: 018, 022, 028, 124
MOVIES: 741.mov

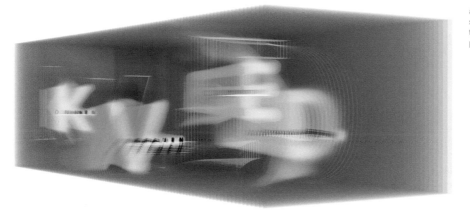

Television advertising clip for an insurance company. Their slogan was integrated as a typographic animation in post-production.

[739]

[740] ⌄   [741.mov/1–2] ›

[741.mov/3]

devk

The television advertising clip for an insurance company was given a typographic animation in the post-production stage.
It was important to ensure that the text was large enough and was displayed for long enough so as to be read. In addition to
the slogan, there was also spoken text which needed to be taken into account. The attention of the viewer was guided by
small tricks. For example, the initial capital of each word always disappeared in the direction from which the next word
appeared. And each word that was faded in was announced by a bright spot. At the moment when the letter has already
appeared in green, an unsharp white dot »moderates« the word in black type.

~ [742/1–2]

[742/3]

[742/4]   [742/5]

telekom

This animation was completely created as a motion graphic and its main layers are abstract elements, albeit with the integration of a few real footage sequences. The structure of this animation and the use of fade-in effects strongly guides the viewer's attention. The major characteristic is the principle of »visual moderation«. The guidance of the eye. Wherever the rectangle zooms out, it zooms in again at the same position with a new element. So the viewer has only to follow the motif.

Wherever there is a fade-out, a fade-in of a new element occurs; where there is a movement to the right, there will be a corresponding movement to the left. And there are hardly any jump cuts.

INFO [Motion graphics for an international brand event. The attention of the viewer is guided by continuous visual »moderation«.]

[739] Volumetric display of individual time slices
[740] Sequence, typographic layer
[741.mov/1–2] Stills from the film
[741.mov/3] Sequences from the film
[742/1–2] Stills from the film
[742/3] Sequence from the film
[742/4–5] Stills from the film

motion graphics

Displacement, motion tracking and manually set key frames determine the dynamics and appearance of this sequence

GRID: 4D grid
PRINCIPLE: Using motion tracking and luminance values as a grid, setting key frames manually
METHOD: Displacing the position of graphical elements
EXAMPLE: Promotional clip
CONTEXT: 022, 038, 088, 124
MOVIE: 743.mov

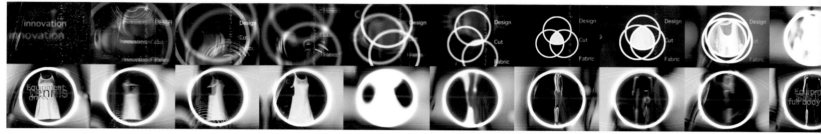

[743.mov/1–2]

adidas

This animation was designed for the introduction of a new marketing concept. Many layers in this sequence were animated manually. Only in isolated cases temporary grids were used. Some partial sequences were created by displacement, others show a linking of the movement paths of individual elements.
The beginning of the animation shows typography which has been deformed through displacement by real footage. In the middle section there are typographic animations which are based on the movements of graphical elements and vice versa. But the initial impulse for the dynamics was generated manually.

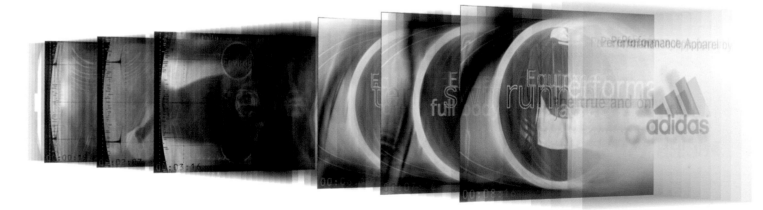

[744]

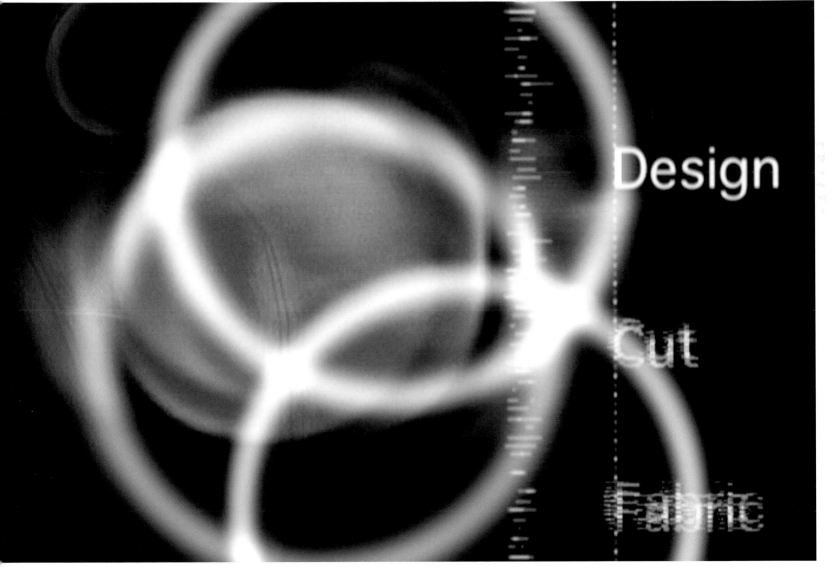

Design

Cut

Fabric

[743.mov/3]

[743.mov/1–2] Sequences from the promotional clip
[744] Volumetric display of individual frames
[743.mov/3] Still from the promotional clip

motion graphics

Four-point tracking and displacement of time and typography determine this sequence

GRID: 3D grid, 4D grid
PRINCIPLE: Using multiple movement points and luminance as grid
METHOD: Tracking of four points in motion and displacing typography
EXAMPLE: Advertising TV clip
CONTEXT: 022, 052, 088, 124
MOVIE: 745.mov

[745.mov/1]

bmp

The idea, concept and implementation of this television spot were based on a playful treatment of the factor of time. The advertising clip for a company with the slogan »Why go with the times if you can be ahead of them?« contains numerous tricks and special effects which had to be already taken into account when the footage was filmed. For example, the main character moves towards the viewer, but all other passers-by move backwards. In the set this was produced exactly the other way round. In post-production, changes of colour were made and numerous preparations for the typographic animation were implemented. To ensure that the type is always legible in spite of the many differences of colour and brightness in the footage, these areas were partially post-edited. Four-point tracking was used to place partial sequences from the clip on a television, which is itself placed in the sequence. This is a classical application of four-point tracking. The tracking serves to adjust the recorded sequence exactly to the object (in this case the television) in spite of the movement of the camera.

INFO [Post-production effects, four-point tracking and displacement of time and typography determine the design of this commercial.]

[745.mov/2]

[745.mov/3]

([746]

[745.mov/4]

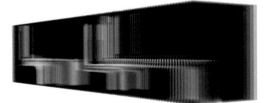

[747]

[745.mov/1–3] Stills from the commercial
[746] Sequence of the typography layer
[745.mov/4] Sequences from the commercial
[747] Volumetric display of the typography layer

motion graphics

Design of the dramaturgy within just a few frames – freestyle
Typography is displaced by the luminance value of graphics

GRID: 3D grid, 4D grid
PRINCIPLE: Using the time frame as grid, using luminance values as grid
METHOD: Freestyle design, displacing typography
EXAMPLE: Logo animation
CONTEXT: 018, 034, 088, 124
MOVIES: 750.mov, 743.mov

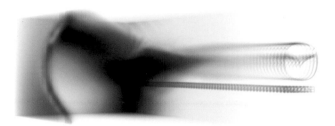

[748]
Designing dramaturgy within 25 frames.

[749]

[750.mov/1]

[750.mov/2]

mazda

These screens show a very short logo trailer. The animated sequence only consists of 25 frames. Within this short period, a dramaturgical effect had to be created. The last frame aimed to show the logo in its original form. This animation is not directly based on a grid. The extremely short time is the factor that sets the framework for the animation.

[751]

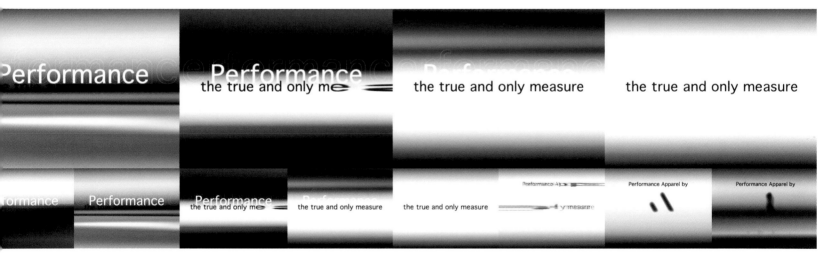

[743.mov/4–5]

adidas

This logo animation is the trailer of an advertising sequence for a marketing concept. It shows the movement of a graphical illustration which consists of unsharp horizontal lines. This illustration is a displacement map which influences the display of the typography and logo and nevertheless remains a visible element of the animation.

[748] Volumetric display of single frames
[749] Volumetric display of single frames
[750.mov/1] End of the logo trailer sequence
[750.mov/2] Extract from the logo trailor sequence
[751] Volumetric display of single frames
[743.mov/4–5] Extract from a logo animation

motion graphics

Logo animation which arises through the manipulation of the properties of a graphic element

GRID: 3D grid, 4D grid
PRINCIPLE: Using graphical element properties as grid
METHOD: Manipulation of graphical element properties, displacing volume
EXAMPLE: Logo animation
CONTEXT: 034, 038, 088, 124
MOVIES: 752.mov, 756.mov

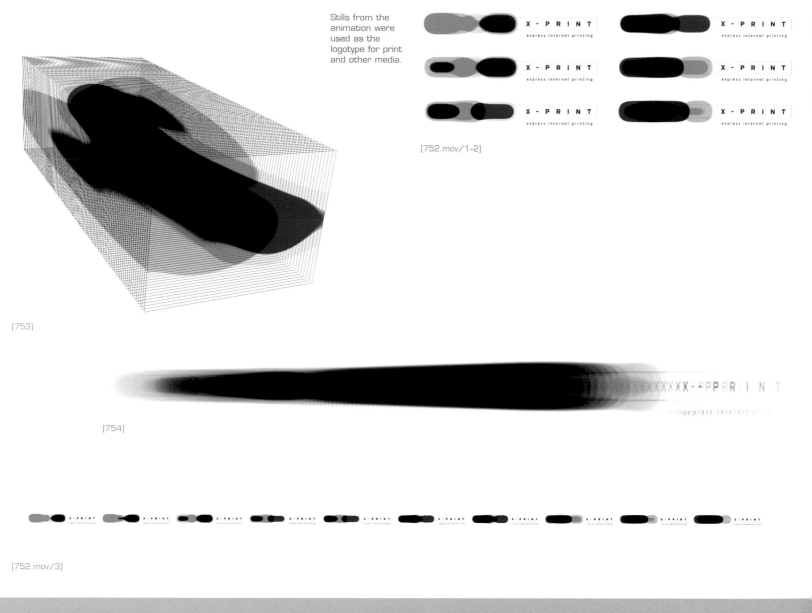

Stills from the animation were used as the logotype for print and other media.

[752.mov/1-2]

[753]

[754]

[752.mov/3]

x-print

This logo animation is based on the manipulation of the properties of a graphic element. On a colour surface, different coloured highlights were set and manually animated so that they moved horizontally in relation to each other. The changes in the colour display due to the increase in the contrasts caused the formation of a black core within the individual elements.

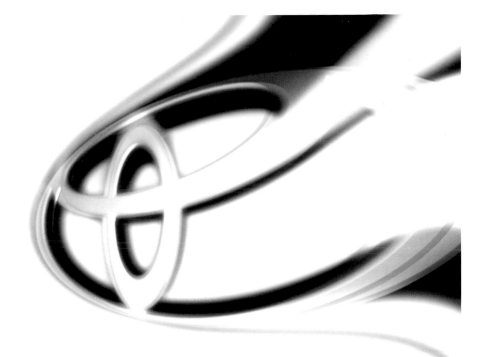

[755]

toyota

In this logo animation, a dynamic 3D grid was used. It deformed the logo in space.

[756.mov/1]

[756.mov/2]

[756.mov/3]

[756.mov/4]

[752.mov/1–2] Stills from the sequence
[753] Volumetric display of single frames
[754] Display of single frames
[752.mov/3] Extract from the sequence
[755] Volumetric display of single frames
[756.mov/1–3] Stills from the sequence
[756.mov/4] Extract from the sequence

motion graphics

>SPATIAL ANIMATION >CHARACTER ANIMATION >TYPOGRAPHY ANIMATION LOGO ANIMATION

Behaviour of graphic elements used as the brand element of cross-media concepts

GRID: 3D grid, 4D grid
PRINCIPLE: Using motion paths as grid
METHOD: Motion tracking of sport
EXAMPLE: Cross-media brand design
CONTEXT: 046, 050, 106, 124
MOVIES: 759.mov, 761.mov

[757]

[758]

Dynamic logo of the Nea Awards 2000. This abstract form is a
visualisation of the dynamics of individual extreme sports. The logo was
adapted to the medium for each sport.

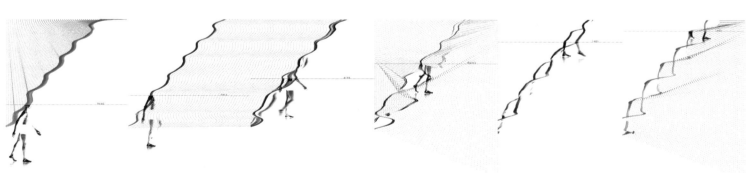

[759.mov]

This illustration shows how the movement sequences of the sporting
participants were transformed to create the graphics shown above. The
movement sequences of the body or of certain limbs were traced with
lines over a considerable time. This made the entire position changes of
these limbs visible in a single image.

v.nea-awards.com/surfing

[760]

[761.mov/1]

nea awards

The Nea Awards, an international competition for extreme sports, was held for the first time in 2000. For this, a cross-media concept was to be developed which would create a visual language across various media. First, adverts were published for a website on which users could select their favourite extreme sports personalities. A live event with the presentation of the prizes was given atmosphere by the appropriate screenings.

The print, Web and TV campaigns were all based on a fundamental idea which could be spelled out by the media and the various sports.

The goal was to develop media-immanent solutions which would exploit the special characteristics of the respective media in a virtuoso and progressive manner. The idea of the visual concept was to analyse and extract the dynamics of the individual sports in order to generate abstract forms, the so-called »shapes«. The principle of this extraction is explained in figure [759.mov]. This very abstract visual language, which was transformed for each medium, aimed to achieve the greatest possible contrast to other publications in the area of extreme sports. The »shapes« show all the characteristic dynamics of a sport in a single image and were designed as eye-catchers.

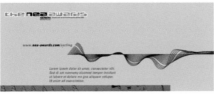

[762]

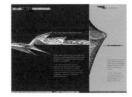

[763]   [764]

[757] Category-specific logo
[758] Category-specific logo
[759.mov] Form development principle
[760] Shape for the »surfing« category
[761.mov/1] Sequence from the event screenings
[762] Advert in print media, landscape format, single page
[763] Advert in print media, portrait format, full page
[764] Advert in print media, portrait format, single page

motion graphics

Behaviour of graphics used as the brand element of cross-media concepts

GRID: 3D grid, 4D grid
PRINCIPLE: Using motion paths as grid
METHOD: Motion tracking of sport
EXAMPLE: Cross-media brand design
CONTEXT: 050, 066, 106, 124
MOVIE: 761.mov

[761.mov/2], [761.mov/3]

[761.mov/4-5]

[765]

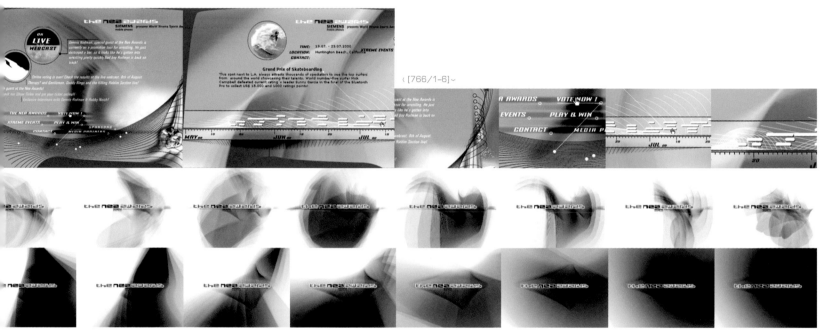

< [766/1–6] ~

[761.mov/6–7]

nea awards

The design of the logo is based on various ideas – the main being the creation of an identity by means of a visual principle. For example, each sport has its own logo; the logos all have the same components, but they always look different because each sport generated a different »shape«. On the other hand, the design was also based on the idea that corporate identity can be founded not only on form, but also on behaviour.

The whole potential of the visual concept becomes clear in the transformation in the third and fourth dimensions. Here, the logo of each sport not only has its own distinctive form, it also shows a difference in movement and dynamics. This correlates subconsciously with the sport itself. When the viewer looks at the image he or she not only decrypts a symbol, but also associates the dynamics with something familiar.

The »shapes« were used on the website as an environment and as navigation. They acted as dynamic structures which could also express their shape and their behaviour. In the voting section of the website, a dynamic moderation function in the navigation ensures that the users are able to elect their sports' personality quickly and easily.

[761.mov/2] Still from the Flash logo animation for the Internet
[761.mov/3] Sequence from the Flash logo animation for the Internet
[761.mov/4–5] Stills from the Flash logo animation for the Internet
[765] Volumetric display of a Flash logo animation
[766/1–6] Screenshots from the Flash website
[761.mov/6–7] Sequences from the Flash logo animation for the Internet

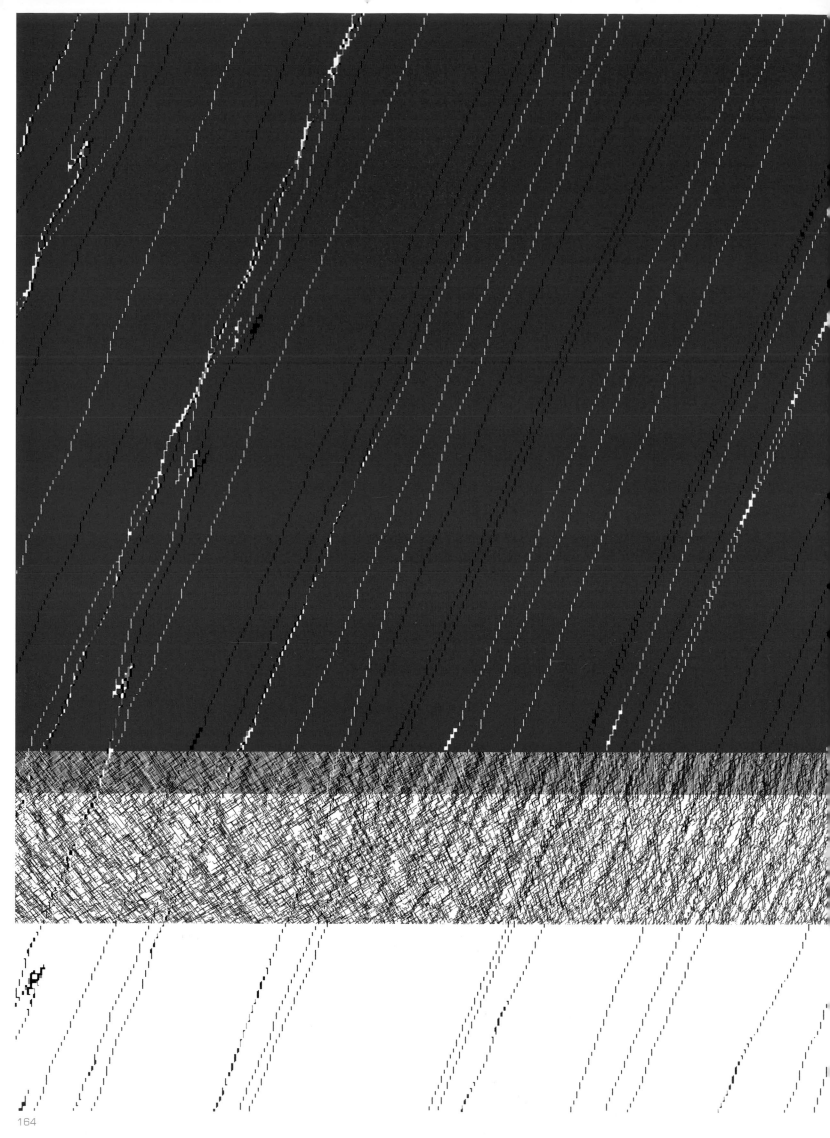

interactive motion

interactive motion

Grids for interactive systems are generally based on the smallest unit, the pixel. Additionally, classic 2D grids are often used, which incorporate descriptions for temporal and interactive sequences as a matrix for the coding. Similar to the field of moving image design, the aim is not to create a solid structure in which to »place« content, but rather the creation of a model that is defined not just by form, but also by behaviour.

If we understand interactive systems as dynamic structures, we can define the designed structure as well as its behaviour as a set of rules, i.e. a grid of the interface. As with complex animations, the set of rules of an interface is defined by its structure, its behaviour and the interaction of all parts. In addition there is the component of usage, the interaction, which means that system behaviour (interfaces) has to be described for all actions of the user. These self-defined rules make possible a quick understanding of functionality and can therefore guarantee a forward-thinking and independent interaction.

In this chapter we introduce the idea of the »navigable structure« as a new principle for the interface. »Navigable structures« are interactive structures that visualise the state of data and its context. They can be directly navigated and individually observed and shaped by the user.

interactive motion

This interface was implemented with various grids. A 4D grid, a functional grid
and a zone grid control the interaction of the interface components

GRID: 2D grid, 4D grid
PRINCIPLE: Design of a »navigable structure«
METHOD: Visualising thematic and temporal relations
EXAMPLE: Online community platform
CONTEXT: 016, 026, 042, 164
MOVIE: –

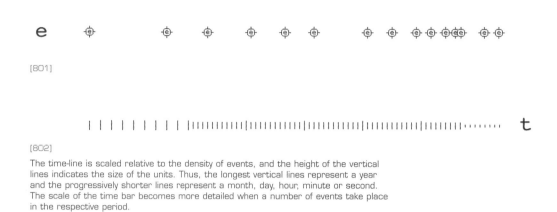

[801]

[802]

The time-line is scaled relative to the density of events, and the height of the vertical
lines indicates the size of the units. Thus, the longest vertical lines represent a year
and the progressively shorter lines represent a month, day, hour, minute or second.
The scale of the time bar becomes more detailed when a number of events take place
in the respective period.

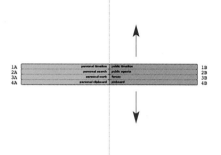

[803]

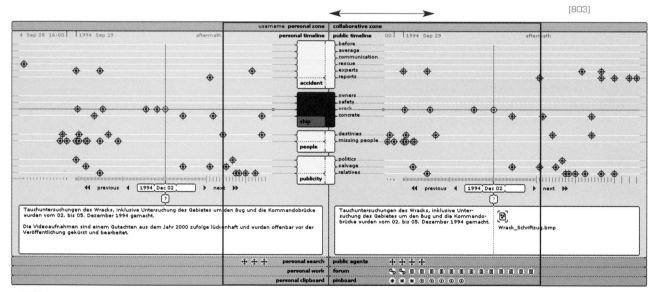

[804]

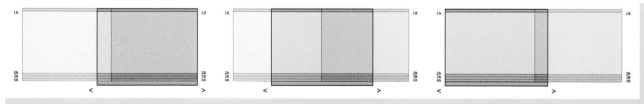

[805/1–3]

[801] Distribution of events
[802] Dynamic calibration of the time-scale
[803] Model of the interface
[804] Overall view of the interface structure
[805/1–3] Views of the interface construction
[806] Subdivision of the time-line into themes, sub-themes and events
[807] Functional layout of the interface
[808] View of the time-line in the public area
[809] View of the agent search in the public area

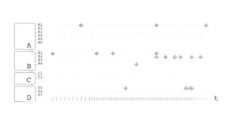

[806]

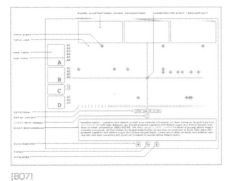

[8071]

Numerous grids are used in this interface: a functional grid which organises the arrangement of the main areas, a zone grid which subdivides the screen into functional units and rules that control the dynamics of the overall structure.

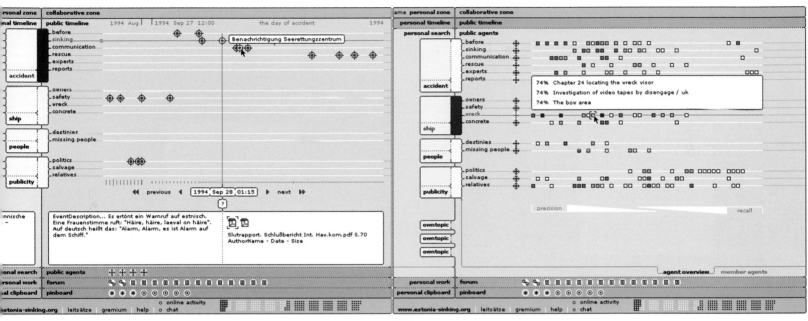

[808]

A relative time grid is used in the area of the time-line. A single display visualises information about specific points in time.

[809]

In the area of the agent search, the results are arranged by the accuracy of the hits on the basis of precision or relevance. And the colour of the sorted squares provides information about the number of documents included.

community platform

This interface for a community platform on the Internet shows a functional principle which is dynamic in several ways. The interface can be moved horizontally to enable the user to decide clearly between the public and the private area. There is a vertical subdivision to separate the interface into the various functional areas: time-line, agents search, forum, bulletin board and cross-system functions.

The structure and behaviour of this interface are geared to the references and links in the content. It thus meets the requirement of creating a maximum of transparency by the direct representation of the data references. A logically exact visualisation of the content and its references aims to give the user an overview of the existing information. The corresponding interaction possibilities offer the maximum possible freedom of navigation.

The application, which deals with a shipwreck that has not yet been solved, combines in its interface numerous forms of representation which are organised into the main themes along the vertical axis. In the first area, the time-line, chronological order is the main criterion for the arrangement and sorting of the content. But it is possible to view the content not only in relation to the point in time, but also by their thematic relevance or by a linear procedure.

The visualisation of the references in the form of lines quickly provides an overview of the thematic reference, the time of the individual events and the associated extra content and documents that can be called up. This »navigable structure« in its present form also provides an overview of the relationships between the components shown, such as events, themes, points in time and existing documents. It can be seen at a glance when much happened in the context of which theme, and when less happened. The user can thus develop an interest for areas of content which may not have appeared relevant without the display of these relationships.

interactive motion

The structural characteristics of a project team, its tasks and the time sequence of the activities in project work
determine the structure and dynamics of this interface

GRID: 3D grid, 4D grid
PRINCIPLE: Design of a »navigable structure«
METHOD: Visualising contextual, structural and temporal relations
EXAMPLE: Interface study for a workflow management tool
CONTEXT: 016, 032, 042, 164
MOVIE: 810.mov

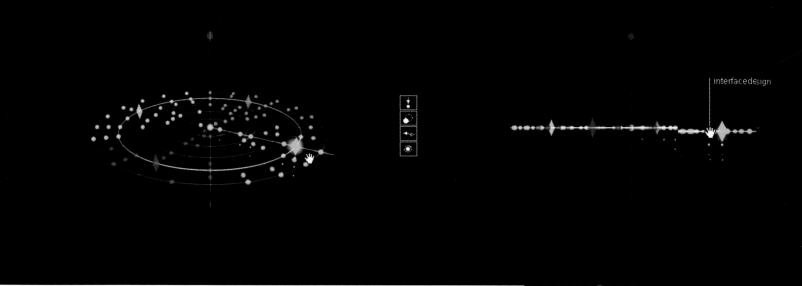

[810.mov/1]   [810.mov/2]

[810.mov/3]   [810.mov/4]   [810.mov/5]

Interior view of interfaces – the position of a user.
The user only sees the documents he or she must
work on.

workflow management tool

This interface is a study for a workflow management system which provides a
pre-defined workflow with all the necessary data and duties which are needed to
handle a specific type of project. It shows an interactive, dynamic structure which
visualises the project participants, the data generated and required and the
project process. The current project status is therefore always visible. If a project
participant does not finish his work within a pre-defined time grid, the
corresponding »workflow node«, which contains the documents needed for this
step of the work begins to shift the concentric arrangement of the time circles.
The delay becomes visible for all participants. The idea was to create a situation
for all parties involved in which they could have a clear picture of their own work
and the status of the total project.

The users can select a view in which they only see their own duties and work
through them, or a view in which they can gain a general impression of the whole
project. To this end, the interface provides both an interior and an exterior view.
Direct links between the content, the person and the time are visualised and dire
made available interactively. The character of the data involved and the need for
individual viewing perspectives for the data were relevant in the design of the interfa

The visualisation of the process in a dynamic structure and the display of this
structure as a »navigable structure«, as we call it, define the organisation. The ru
which created the form of this interface are determined by content relations, inte
dependencies and by the progress of the processes. The structure itself is the gr

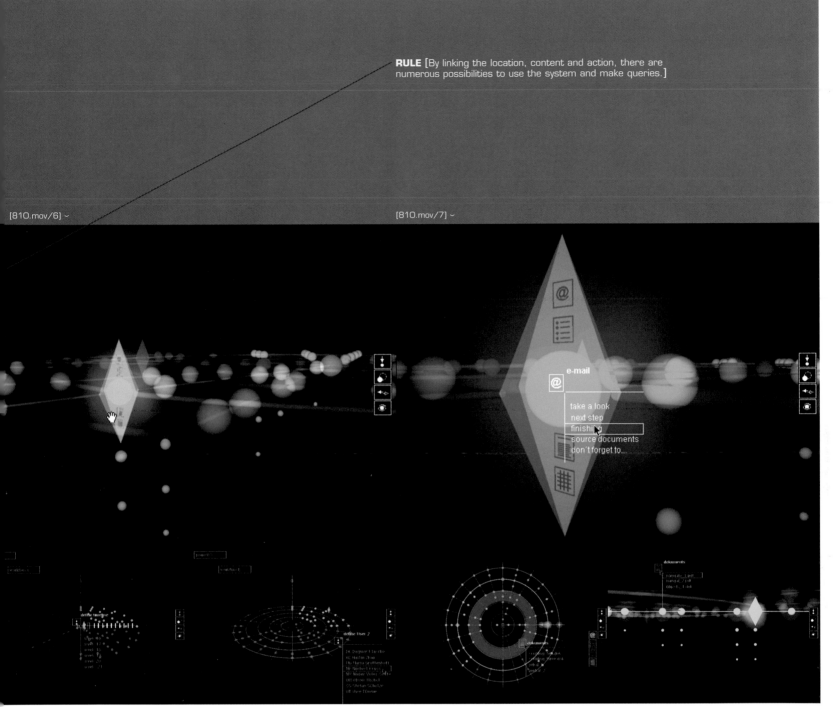

RULE [By linking the location, content and action, there are numerous possibilities to use the system and make queries.]

[810.mov/6] ~

[810.mov/7] ~

e-mail

take a look
next step
finishing
source documents
don´t forget to...

[810.mov/8]   [810.mov/9]   [810.mov/10]   [810.mov/11]

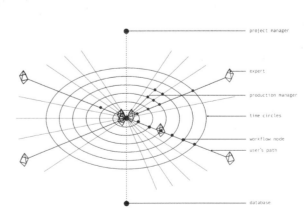

Functional model with all components of the interface.

project manager
expert
production manager
time circles
workflow node
user's path

database

[811]

[810.mov/1] Action: Moving/navigating the structure
[810.mov/2] Action: Query for the milestones
[810.mov/3–5] Interior view of a workflow node
[810.mov/6] Action: Zoom in on the current workflow node
[810.mov/7] Action: Query for related emails
[810.mov/8] Action: Define the time period for the project
[810.mov/9] Action: Define the staff for the project
[810.mov/10] Action: Query for the documents created in one week
[810.mov/11] Action: Query for the documents created in the selected workflow node
[811] Functional model of the interface

interactive motion

The social relationships and the frequency of communication between the sender and recipient within computer-assisted systems determine the structure and dynamics of this interface

GRID: 3D grid, 4D grid
PRINCIPLE: Using interrelations of a communication process as grid
METHOD: Visualising relations, creating a »navigable structure«
EXAMPLE: Interface study for a communication tool »PAM«
CONTEXT: 016, 032, 042, 164
MOVIE: –

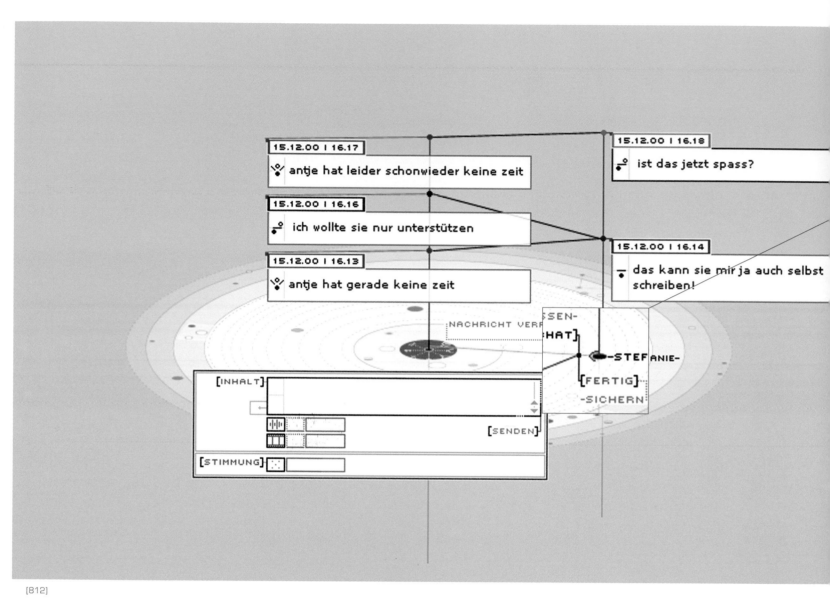

[812]

communication tool

The structure of this interface study is determined by social relationships and the frequency of communication between the user and his discussion partners. The interface subdivides the relationships between discussion partners into social groups and portrays them in the form of concentric circles. The user of this software is represented in the centre of the interface. There, all the necessary tools for communication and organisation are offered. Each participant in the communication is also represented by a circle. The size of the circles shows the amount of data they contain, the position of the circles shows the frequency of the communication. The individual slices of the circle to visualise the social groups are dynamic, so that individual areas can be opened or minimised.

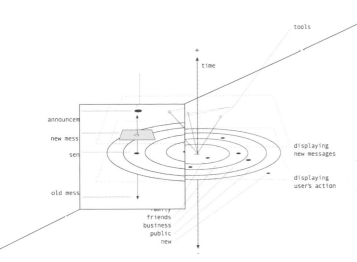

INFO [Status during a chat. It shows the communication partner (Stefanie) and the arrangement of the dialogue along the time axis.]

[813]

The functional model visualises the structure of the interface. The model resulted from the components, processes and functions structured and their relationship to each other and among themselves.

This interface study contains different grids, each of which is responsible for parts of the interface. For example, there is a time structure which can be understood vertically either through the centre of the system, i.e. the representation of the user, or through the centre of the discussion participants represented. This permits a temporal view of all messages which relates either to the sender's messages or the recipient's messages.

There is also a grid which defines the behaviour of messages. Depending on how important the sender has marked a message, the icon informing the recipient of this message will move either quickly or slowly.

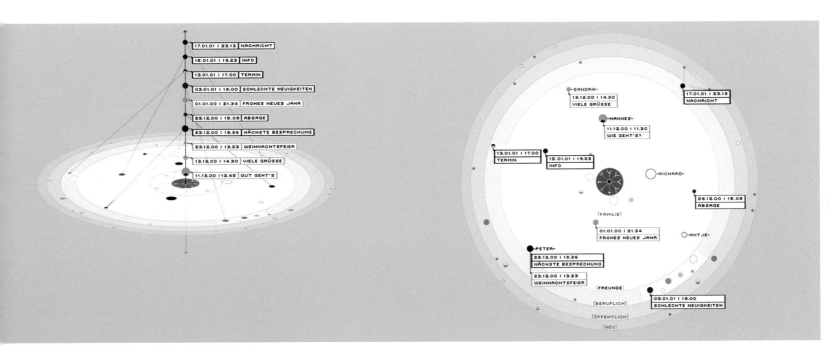

[814]

[815]

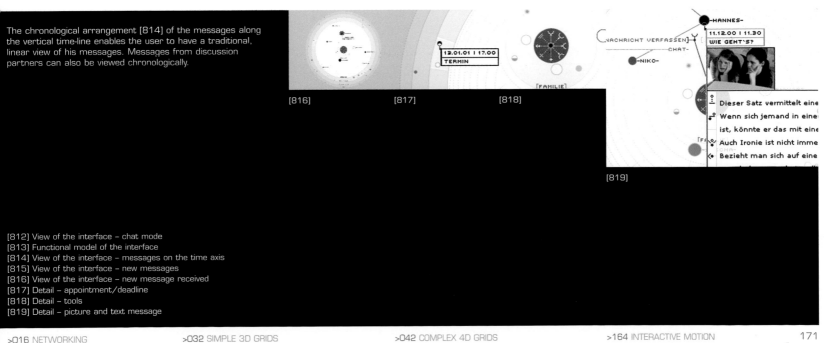

The chronological arrangement [814] of the messages along the vertical time-line enables the user to have a traditional, linear view of his messages. Messages from discussion partners can also be viewed chronologically.

[816]

[817]

[818]

[819]

[812] View of the interface – chat mode
[813] Functional model of the interface
[814] View of the interface – messages on the time axis
[815] View of the interface – new messages
[816] View of the interface – new message received
[817] Detail – appointment/deadline
[818] Detail – tools
[819] Detail – picture and text message

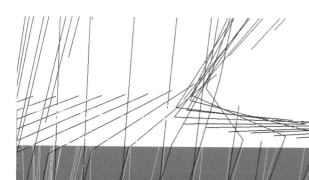

index

index

movie index

movie index

acknowledgements

acknowledgements

We would like to thank the following people for their help and involvement in this project:

Brian Morris for his patience and the possibility to write this book
Natalia Price-Cabrera for her editorial guidance and hard work
Veruschka Götz for her support with communication and organisation
Julia Dietsch for her faith in the project and proofreading of the texts
Claudia Lippert for providing the interface study on communication
Detlef Warning for programming the movie browser
pReview for the temporary taking over of the day-to-day organisation

Tanja Diezmann & Tobias Gremmler